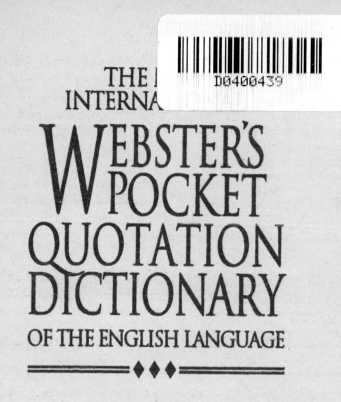

THE NEW
INTERNATIONAL

WEBSTER'S POCKET QUOTATION DICTIONARY

OF THE ENGLISH LANGUAGE

◆◆◆

TRIDENT PRESS
INTERNATIONAL

Published by
Trident Press International
2000 EDITION
Reprinted 2001

ISBN 1-888777-50-8

Printed in Australia

Ability

Natural abilities are like natural plants, that need pruning by study.

Francis Bacon

No amount of ability is of the slightest avail without honor.

Andrew Carnegie

I add this also, that natural ability without education has oftener raised man to glory and virtue than education without natural ability.

Cicero

Ability hits the mark where presumption overshoots and diffidence falls short.

Nicholas of Cusa

Skill to do comes of doing.

Ralph Waldo Emerson

There is something that is much more scarce, something finer far, something rarer than ability. It is the ability to recognize ability.

Elbert Green Hubbard

Better be proficient in one art than a smatterer in a hundred.

Japanese Proverb

A man who qualifies himself well for his calling, never fails of employment.

Thomas Jefferson

Without the assistance of natural capacity, rules and precepts are of no efficacy.

Quintilian

Ability

It is a great ability to be able to conceal one's ability.
François de la Rochefoucauld

The ability to deal with people is as purchasable a commodity as sugar or coffee. And I pay more for that ability than for any other under the sun.
John Davison Rockefeller

So long as a man imagines that he cannot do this or that, so long is he determined not to do it; and consequently so long is it impossible to him that he should do it.

Benedict Spinoza

They are able because they think they are able.

Vergil

Absence

Absence makes the heart grow fonder:
Isle of Beauty, fare thee well!
Thomas Haynes Bayly

But ay the tear comes in me ee,
To think on him that's far awa.

Robert Burns

Our hours in love have wings; in absence crutches.
Colley Cibber

To him that absent is
All things succeed amiss

Cervantes

Friends, though absent, are still present.

Cicero

Absence

Absence from whom we love is worse than death
And frustrate hope severer than despair

William Cowper

Love reckons hours for months, and days for years;
And every little absence is an age.

John Dryden

The absent are never without fault.
Nor the present without excuse.

Benjamin Franklin

Out of sight, out of mind

Homer

Friendship, like love, is destroyed by long absence,
though it may be increased by short intermissions.

Samuel Johnson

But 0 the heavy change, now thou art gone,
Now thou art gone, and never must return!

John Milton

Two evils, monstrous either one apart
Possessed me, and were long and loath at going:
A cry of Absence, Absence, in the heart,
And in the wood the furious winter blowing.

John Crowe Ransom

Absence lessens weak and increases violent passions,
as wind extinguishes tapers and lights up a fire.

Duc François de La Rochefoucauld

Hast thou no care of me? shall I abide
In this dull world, which in thy absence is
No better than a sty?

Shakespeare

Absence

The lord watch between me and thee,
when we are absent from one another.

Genesis 31:49

Greater things are believed of those who are absent.

Tacitus

Action

I am perplexed . . . whether to act or not to act.

Aeschylus

Of every noble action the intent
Is to give worth reward, vice punishment.

Francis Beaumont

The end of man is action, and not thought,
though it be of the noblest.

Thomas Carlyle

I do not believe in a fate that falls on men however
they act; but I do believe in a fate that falls on them
unless they act.

G. K. Chesterton

We should not be so taken up in the search for truth,
as to neglect the needful duties of active life; for it is
only action that gives a true value and commendation
to virtue.

Cicero

A man who waits to believe in action before acting is
anything you like, but he's not a man of action. It is
as if a tennis player before returning a ball stopped to
think about his views of the physical and mental advantages of tennis. You must act as you breathe.

Georges Clemenceau

Action

When a man asks himself what is meant by action he proves that he isn't a man of action. Action is a lack of balance. In order to act you must be somewhat insane. A reasonably sensible man is satisfied with thinking.

Georges Clemenceau

Deliberate with caution, but act with decision; and yield with graciousness, or oppose with firmness.

Charles Caleb Colton

Action may not always bring happiness; but there is no happiness without action.

Benjamin Disraeli

A man's action is only a picture book of his creed.

Ralph Waldo Emerson

Brave actions never want a Trumpet.

Thomas Fuller

Mark this well, you proud men of action!
you are, after all nothing but unconscious
instruments of the men of thought.

Heinrich Heine

I find the great thing in this world is not so much where we stand, as in what direction we are moving. To reach the port of heaven, we must sail sometimes with the wind and sometimes against it,
—but we must sail, and not drift, nor lie at anchor.

Oliver Wendell Holmes

The great end of life is not knowledge, but action.

T. H. Huxley

Actions speak louder than words.

Proverb

Action

With a good conscience our only sure reward, with history the final judge of our deeds, let us go forth to lead the land we love, asking His blessing and His help, but knowing that here on earth God's work must truly be our own.

John F. Kennedy

Each time a man stands up for an ideal, or acts to improve the lot of others, or strikes out against injustice, he sends forth a tiny ripple of hope, and...
...those ripples build a current which can sweep down the mightiest walls of oppression and resistance.

Robert F. Kennedy

You will be better advised to watch what we do instead of what we say.

John N. Mitchell

We would often be ashamed of our finest actions if the world understood all the motives which produced them.

François de la Rochefoucauld

We are face to face with our destiny and we must meet it with a high and resolute courage. For us is the life of action, of strenuous performance of duty; let us live in the harness, striving mightily; let us rather run the risk of wearing out than rusting out.

Theodore Roosevelt

Things won are done, joy's soul lies in the doing.

Shakespeare

One hour of life, crowded to the full with glorious action, and filled with noble risks, is worth whole years of those mean observances of paltry decorum.

Walter Scott

If it were done when 'tis done, then 'twere well
It were done quickly.

Shakespeare

Heaven n'er helps the men who will not act.

Sophocles

A rolling stone can gather no moss.

Publilius Syrus

No sooner said than done.

Terence

We cannot think first and act afterwards. From the moment of birth we are immersed in action, and can only fitfully guide it by taking thought.

Alfred North Whitehead

Bullfight critics row on row
Crowd the vast arena full
But only one man's there who knows
And he's the man who fights the bull

Anonymous

Adversity

The virtue of prosperity is temperance; the virtue of adversity is fortitude. . . .

Francis Bacon

Hope and patience are two sovereign remedies for all, the surest reposals, the softest cushions to lean on in adversity.

Robert Burton

Adversity is the first path to truth.

George Gordon, Lord Byron

Adversity

Adversity is sometimes hard upon a man; but for one man who can stand prosperity there are a hundred that will stand adversity.

Thomas Carlyle

Friendship, of itself a holy tie,
Is made more sacred by adversity.

John Dryden

In time of prosperity friends will be plenty;
In time of adversity not one in twenty.

James Howell

Adversity has the effect of eliciting talents which in prosperous circumstances would have lain dormant.

Horace

The flower that follows the sun does so even in cloudy days.

Robert Leighton

Who hath not known ill fortune, never knew himself, or his own virtue.

David Mallet

Mishaps are like knives, that either serve us or cut us, as we grasp them by the blade or the handle.

Herman Melville

In adversity a man is saved by hope.

Menander

It is a kingly action, believe me, to come to the help of those who are fallen.

Ovid

Trial is the true test of mortal men.

Pindar

Of one ill comes many.

Scottish proverb

Great men rejoice in adversity just as brave soldiers triumph in war.

Seneca

Sweet are the uses of adversity,
Which like the toad, ugle and venomous,
Wears yet a precious jewel in his head.

Shakespeare

The worst is not
So long as we can say, "This is the worst."

Shakespeare

It is the duty of all persons, when affairs are the most prosperous, then in especial to reflect within themselves in what way they are to endure adversity.

Terence

In the day of prosperity be joyful, but in the day of adversity consider.

Ecclesiastes 8

A friend loveth at all times, and a brother is born for adversity.

Proverbs 17:17

Advice

Never give advice in a crowd.

Arabian Proverb

The worst men often give the best advice.

Philip James Bailey

A fool sometimes gives weighty advice.

Nicholas Boileau

Advice

Who cannot give good counsel? 'Tis cheap, it costs them nothing.

Robert Burton

A woman's advice is not worth much,
but he who doesn't heed it is a fool.

Pedro Calderón

No one can give you better advice than yourself.

Cicero

We ask advice, but we mean approbation.

Charles C. Colton

Advice is least heeded when most needed.

English Proverb

Don't give your advice before you are called upon.

Desiderius Erasmus

'Tis easier to advise the suffering than to bear suffering.

Euripides

They that will not be counselled, cannot be helped. If you do not hear reason she will rap you on the knuckles.

Benjamin Franklin

Unasked advice is a trespass on sacred privacy.

Henry Stanley Haskins

Whatever advice you give, be short.

Horace

Advice is offensive, --because it shows us that we are known to others as well as to ourselves.

Samuel Johnson

Advice is seldom welcome.
Those who need it most, like it least.

Samuel Johnson

When Thales was asked what was difficult, he said,
  "To know one's self."
And what was easy, "To advise another."

Diogenes Laertius

Never advise anyone to go to war or to marry.

Spanish Proverb

Many receive advice, only the wise profit by it.

Publilius Syrus

The only thing to do with good advice is to pass it on.
It is never of any use to oneself.

Oscar Wilde

Age

Age appears to be the best in four things—old wood
best to burn, old wine to drink, old friends to trust,
and old authors to read.

Francis Bacon

He lives long that lives till all are weary of him.

Henry George Bohn

Grow old along with me!
The best is yet to be,
The last of life,
  for which the first was made.

Robert Browning

Let age approve of youth,
  and death complete the same.

Robert Browning

Age

We hope to grow old, and we fear old age:
  that is to say, we love life and flee death.
Jean de la Bruyère

Yet somehow our society must make it right and possible for old people not to fear the young or be deserted by them, for the test of a civilization is in the way that is cares for its helpless members.
Pearl S. Buck

Young men think old men are fools; but old men *know* young men are fools.
George Chapman

Old age isn't so bad when you consider the alternative.
Attributed to Maurice Chevalier

I am ready to meet my Maker. Whether my Maker is prepared for the great ordeal of meeting me is another matter.
Winston Churchill

For as I like a young man in whom there is something of the old, so I like an old man in whom there is something of the young.
Cicero

No one is so old as to think he cannot live one more year.
Cicero

A man is as old as he's feeling
A woman as old as she looks.
Mortimer Collins

Folly in youth is sin, in age is madness.
Samuel Daniel

Age is like love; it cannot be hid.

Thomas Dekker

Youth is a blunder; Manhood a struggle;
Old Age a regret.

Benjamin Disraeli

A woman is as old as she looks to a man that likes to look at her.

Finley Peter Dunne

Age does not depend upon years, but upon temperament and health. Some men are born old, and some never grow so.

Tryon Edwards

We do not count a man's years until he has nothing else to count.

Ralph Waldo Emerson

Forty is the old age of youth;
   fifty is the youth of old age.

Victor Hugo

Whenever a man's friends begin to compliment him about looking young, he may be sure that they think he is growing old.

Washington Irving

To the old cat give a tender mouse.

Italian Proverb

It was near a miracle to see an old man silent, since talking is the disease of age.

Ben Jonson

Growing old is no more than a bad habit which a busy man has no time to form

André Maurois

Age

Of middle age the best that can be said is that a middle-aged person has likely learned how to have a little fun in spite of his troubles.

Don Marquis

He who is of a calm and happy nature will hardly feel the pressure of Age, but to him who is of an opposite disposition, youth and age are equally a burden.

Plato

He whom the gods favour dies in youth.

Plautus

When men grow virtuous in old age, they only make a sacrifice to God of the devil's leavings.

Alexander Pope

As one grows older,
   one becomes wiser and more foolish

François de la Rochefoucauld

Before old age my care was to live well;
in old age, to die well.

Seneca

Age cannot wither her, nor custom stale
Her infinite variety.

Shakespeare

Nobody loves life like an old man.

Sophocles

In the days of my youth I remembered my God,
And He hath not forgotten my age.

Robert Southey

We are always the same age inside.

Gertrude Stein

To hold the same views at forty as we held at twenty is to have been stupefied for a score of years, and take rank, not as a prophet, but as an untouchable brat, well birched and none the wiser.

Robert Louis Stevenson

No wise man ever wished to be younger.

Jonathan Swift

To love is natural in a young man, a shame in an old one.

Publilius Syrus

A fool at forty is a fool indeed.

Edward Young

Agriculture

For of all gainful professions, nothing is better, nothing more pleasing, nothing more delightful, nothing better becomes a well-bred man than agriculture.

Cicero

Man has only a thin layer of soil between himself and starvation.

Attributed to Bard of Cincinnati

Alcohol

At the third cup, wine drinks the man.

Hokekyô Sho

Were I to commence my administration again, . . . the first question I would ask respecting a candidate would be, "Does he use ardent spirits?"

Attributed to Thomas Jefferson

Alcohol

I believe, if we take habitual drunkards as a class, their heads and their hearts will bear an advantageous comparison with those of any other class.

Abraham Lincoln

Ambition

The slave has but one master; the man of ambition has as many as there are people useful to his fortune.

Jean de la Bruyère

It is attempting to reach the top at a single leap, that so much misery is caused in the world.

William Cobbett

All ambitions are lawful except those which climb upward on the miseries or credulities of mankind.

Joseph Conrad

'Tis a laudable Ambition, that aims at being better than his Neighbours.

Ben Franklin

Every eel hopes to become a whale.

German Proverb

A man without ambition is like a woman without beauty.

Frank Harris

Ambition is not a weakness unless it be disproportioned to the capacity. To have more ambition than ability is to be at once weak and unhappy.

George Stillman Hillard

Ambition and suspicion always go together.

Georg Christoph Lichtenberg

Where ambition can cover its enterprises, even to the person himself, under the appearance of principle, it is the most incurable and inflexible of passions.

David Hume

Most people would succeed in small things if they were not troubled by great ambitions.

Henry Wadsworth Longfellow

The same ambition can destroy or save,
And makes a patriot as it makes a knave.

Alexander Pope

Ambition is a vice, but it may be the father of virtue.

Quintilian

The very substance of the ambitious is merely the shadow of a dream.

Shakespeare

America

America, thou half-brother of the world; With something good and bad of every land.

Philip James Bailey

America is the country where you buy a lifetime supply of aspirin for one dollar and use it up in two weeks.

John Barrymore

America has believed that in differentiation, not in uniformity, lies the path of progress. It acted on this belief; it has advanced human happiness, and it has prospered.

Louis Dembitz Brandeis

America

America is the only nation in history which miraculously has gone directly from barbarism to degeneration without the usual interval of civilization.
Attributed to Georges Clemenceau

The metaphor of the melting pot is unfortunate and misleading. A more accurate analogy would be a salad bowl, for, though the salad is an entity, the lettuce can still be distinguished from the chicory, the tomatoes from the cabbage.
Carl N. Degler

Good Americans, when they die, go to Paris.
Oliver Wendell Holmes

I am willing to love all mankind, except an American.
Samuel Johnson

The surface of American society is covered with a layer of democratic paint, but from time to time one can see the old aristocratic colors breaking through.
Alexis de Tocqueville

The Americans, like the English, probably make love worse than any other race.
Walt Whitman

Anger

I was angry with my friend:
I told my wrath, my wrath did end.
I was angry with my foe;
I told it not, my wrath did grow.

William Blake

Anger begins with folly and ends with repentance.
Henry George Bohn

Violence in the voice is often only the death rattle of reason in the throat.

John Frederick Boyes

Truly to moderate your mind and speech when you are angry, or else to hold your peace, betokens no ordinary nature.

Cicero

When anger rises, think of the consequences.

Confucius

Beware the fury of a patient man.

John Dryden

Anger and folly walk cheek by jowl;
repentance treads on both their heels.

Benjamin Franklin

Two things a man should never be angry at: what he can help, and what he cannot help.

Thomas Fuller

Anger is a sort of madness and the noblest causes have been damaged by advocates affected with temporary lunacy,

Mahatma Gandhi

Temper: a quality that, at critical moments, brings out the best in steel and the worst in people.

Oscar Hammling

Let anger's fire be slow to burn.

George Herbert

The best answer to anger is silence.

German Proverb

Anger

When I am angry I can write, pray, and preach well, for then my whole temperament is quickened, my understanding sharpened, and all mundane vexations and temptations depart.

Martin Luther

A soft answer turneth away wrath; but grievous words stir up anger.

Proverbs 15:1

He best keeps from anger who remembers that God is always looking upon him.

Plato

Anger begins in folly, and ends in repentance.

Pythagoras

Animals

And for these also, Dear Lord, the humble beasts, who with us bear the burden and heat of the day, and offer their guileless lives for the well-being of their country, we supplicate Thy great tenderness of heart, for Thou hast promised to save both man and beast. And great is Thy loving kindness, Oh Master, Savior of the world.

Attributed to St. Basil of Caesarea

To my way of thinking there's something wrong, or missing, with any person who hasn't got a soft spot in their heart for an animal of some kind.

Will James

Architecture

The stone which the builders refused is become the head stone of the corner.

Psalms 118:22

Architecture has its political Use; publick Buildings being the Ornament of a Country; it establishes a Nation, draws People and Commerce; makes the People love their native Country, which Passion is the Original of all great Actions in a Common-wealth . . . Architecture aims at Eternity.

Christopher Wren

Art

Art, as far as it has the ability, follows nature, as a pupil imitates his master, so that art must be, as it were, a descendant of God.

Dante Alighieri

Never judge a work of art by its defects.

Washington Allston

It is the glory and good of Art;
That Art remains the one way possible
Of speaking truth. . . .

Robert Browning

An artist cannot speak about his art any more than a plant can discuss horticulture.

Jean Cocteau

Art imitates nature as well as it can, as a pupil follows his master; thus is it a sort of grandchild of God.

Dante

In life beauty perishes, but not in art.

Leonardo da Vinci

Art

Art is the stored honey of the human soul gathered on wings of misery and travail.

Theodore Dreiser

In sculpture did any one ever call the Apollo a fancy piece; or say of the Laocoön how it might be made different? A masterpiece of art has, to the mind, a fixed place in the chain of being, as much as a plant or a crystal.

Ralph Waldo Emerson

Great art is the contempt of a great man for small art.

F. Scott Fitzgerald

Nobody, I think, ought to read poetry, or look at pictures or statues, who cannot find a great deal more in them than the poet or artist has actually expressed.

Nathaniel Hawthorne

Rules and models destroy genius and art.

William Hazlitt

Life is short, the art long, opportunity fleeting, experience treacherous, judgment difficult.

Hippocrates

Art may make a suit of clothes; but Nature must produce a man.

David Hume

The mission of art is to represent nature; not to imitate her.

William Morris Hunt

Art is nothing more than the shadow of humanity.

Henry James

Art hath an enemy called ignorance.

Ben Jonson

There is a connection, hard to explain logically but easy to feel, between achievement in public life and progress in the arts.

John F. Kennedy

The more minimal the art, the more maximum the explanation.

Hilton Kramer

The true work of art is but a shadow of the divine perfection.

Michelangelo

To have faithfully studied the honorable arts, softens the manners and keeps them free from harshness.

Ovid

There are three arts which are concerned with all things: one which uses, another which makes, and a third which imitates them.

Plato

True artists are almost the only men who do their work with pleasure.

Auguste Rodin

The artist is the only man who knows what to do with beauty.

Jean Rostand

When love and skill work together expect a masterpiece.

John Ruskin

Art

An artist may visit a museum, but only a pedant can live there.

George Santayana

Art is not a handicraft; it is the transmission of feeling the artist has experienced.

Leo Tolstoy

A work of art is a corner of creation seen through a temperament.

Émile Zola

Autumn

Autumn wins you best by this, its mute
Appeal to sympathy for its decay.

Robert Browning

All-cheering Plenty, with her flowing horn,
Led yellow Autumn, wreath'd with nodding corn.

Robert Burns

The melancholy days are come,
   the saddest of the year,
Of wailing winds, and naked woods,
   and meadows brown and sear.

William Cullen Bryant

She loves the bare, the withered tree;
She walks the sodden pasture lane.

Robert Frost

Dread autumn, harvest-season of the Goddess of Death.

Horace

A solemn land of long-fulfilled desires
Is this, and year by year the self-same fires
Burn in the trees.

Mary Webb

Avarice

Be not penny-wise; riches have wings, and sometimes
they fly away of themselves, sometimes they must be
set flying to bring in more.

Francis Bacon

If you would abolish avarice, you must abolish its
mother, luxury.

Cicero

Avarice, in old age, is foolish; for what can be more
absurd than to increase our provisions for the road
the nearer we approach to our journey's end?

Cicero

Would'st thou both eat thy cake and have it?

George Herbert

It is sheer madness to live in want in order to be
wealthy when you die.

Juvenal

The beautiful eyes of my money-box!
He speaks of it as a lover of his mistress.

Molière

They are greedy dogs which can never have enough.

Isaiah 56:11

Avarice

The lust of avarice has so totally seized upon mankind that their wealth seems rather to possess them, than they to possess their wealth.

Pliny the Elder

Bank

A bank is a place where they lend you an umbrella in fair weather and ask for it back again when it begins to rain.

Robert Frost

Banking establishments are more dangerous than standing armies.

Thomas Jefferson

Beauty

Beauty and wisdom are seldom found together.

Petronius Arbiter

Beauty is the gift of God.

Aristotle

There is no excellent beauty that hath not some strangeness in the proportion.

Francis Bacon

An appearance of delicacy, and even of fragility, is almost essential to beauty.

Edmund Burke

It is the beautiful bird that gets caged.

Chinese Proverb

Beauty is not caused. It is.

Emily Dickinson

Zest is the secret of all beauty. There is no beauty that is attractive without zest.

Christian Dior

No Spring, nor Summer beauty hath such grace,
As I have seen in one Autumnal face.

John Donne

True beauty consists in purity of heart.

Mahatma Gandhi

Beauty is in the eye of the beholder.

Margaret W. Hungerford

A thing of beauty is a joy forever;
Its loveliness increases; it will never
Pass into nothingness. . . .

John Keats

"Beauty is truth, truth beauty," that is all
Ye know on earth, and all ye need to know.

John Keats

I look forward to an America which will not be afraid of grace and beauty.

John F. Kennedy

Euclid alone
Has looked on Beauty bare.

Edna St. Vincent Millay

[On vanity:] The nose of Cleopatra: if it had been shorter, the face of the earth would have changed.

Blaise Pascal

Beauty provoketh thieves sooner than gold.

Shakespeare

O how can beautie maister the most strong!

Edmund Spenser

Belief

Believe nothing, O monks, merely because you have been told it... or because it is traditional, or because you yourselves have imagined it. Do not believe what your teacher tells you merely out of respect for the teacher. But whatsoever, after due examination and analysis, you find to be conducive to the good, the benefit, the welfare of all beings—that doctrine believe and cling to, and take it as your guide.

Attributed to Buddha

Give to us clear vision that we may know where to stand and what to stand for—because unless we stand for something, we shall fall for anything.

Peter Marshall

What counts now is not just what we are against, but what we are for. Who leads us is less important than what leads us—what convictions, what courage, what faith—win or lose.

Adlai E. Stevenson

Best

I do the very best I know how--the very best I can; and I mean to keep doing so until the end. If the end brings me out all right, what is said against me won't amount to anything. If the end brings me out wrong, ten angels swearing I was right would make no difference.

Abraham Lincoln

I am as bad as the worst but, thank God, I am as good as the best.

Walt Whitman

In this best of all possible worlds, My Lord the Baron's castle was the finest of castles, and My Lady the best of all possible Baronesses. "It is demonstrated," [Pangloss] said, "that things cannot be otherwise, for, everything being made for an end, everything is necessarily for the best end."

Voltaire

Betrayal

On this tenth day of June, 1940, the hand that held the dagger has struck it into the back of its neighbor.

Franklin D. Roosevelt

Blood

I am in blood
Stepp'd in so far that, should I wade no more,
Returning were as tedious as go o'er

Shakespeare

A conscientious man would be cautious how he dealt in blood

Edmund Burke

I have nothing to offer but blood, toil, tears and sweat.

Winston Churchill

Books

That is a good book which is opened with expectation, and closed with delight and profit.

Amos Bronson Alcott

Books

Some books are to be tasted; others swallowed; and some few to be chewed and digested.

Francis Bacon

The man who does not read good books has no advantage over the man who can't read them.

Mark Twain

The world of books is the most remarkable creation of man. Nothing else that he builds ever lasts. Monuments fall; nations perish; civilizations grow old and die out; and, after an era of darkness, new races build others. But in the world of books are volumes that have seen this happen again and again, and yet live on, still young, still as fresh as the day they were written, still telling men's hearts of the hearts of men centuries dead.

Clarence S. Day

Books are the quietest and most constant of friends; they are the most accessible and wisest of counsellors, and the most patient of teachers.

Charles W. Eliot

All good books are alike in that they are truer than if they had really happened and after you are finished reading one you will feel that all that happened to you and afterwards it all belongs to you; the good and the bad, the ecstacy, the remorse and sorrow, the people and the places and how the weather was.

Ernest Hemingway

Books are good enough in their own way, byt they are a mighty bloodless substitute for life.

Robert Louis Stevenson

Brotherhood

Our doctrine of equality and liberty and humanity comes from our belief in the brotherhood of man, through the fatherhood of God.

Calvin Coolidge

There is a destiny that makes us brothers:
None goes his way alone:
All that we send into the lives of others
Comes back onto our own.

Edwin Markham

Humanity cannot go forward, civilization cannot advance, except as the philosophy of force is replaced by that of human brotherhood.

Francis Bowes Sayre

Business

We should keep in mind that the humanities come before the dollars. Our first duty runs to man before business, but we must not forget that sometimes the two are interchangeable.

Bernard Baruch

The gambling known as business looks with austere disfavor upon the business known as gambling.

Ambrose Gwinnett Bierce

The goals of business are inseparable from the goals of the whole community. Every attempt to sever the organic unity of business and the community inflicts equal hardship on both.

Earl Bunting

Business

The substance of the eminent Socialist gentleman's speech is that making a profit is a sin, but it is my belief that the real sin is taking a loss.

Winston Churchill

The trusts and combinations--the communism of pelf--whose machinations have prevented us from reaching the success we deserved, should not be forgotten nor forgiven.

Grover Cleveland

After all, the chief business of the American people is business.

Calvin Coolidge

I do not believe government can run any business as efficiently as private enterprise, and the victim of every such experiment is the public.

Thomas E. Dewey

All business proceeds on beliefs, or judgments of probabilities, and not on certainties.

Charles William Eliot

So the question is, do *corporate executives,* provided they stay within the law, have responsibilities in their business activities other than to make as much money for their stockholders as possible? And my answer to that is, no they do not.

Milton Friedman

We are obviously all hurt by inflation. Everybody is hurt by inflation. If you really wanted to examine who percentage-wise is hurt the most in their incomes, it is the Wall Street brokers. I mean their incomes have gone down the most.

Alan Greenspan

The man who makes an appearance in the business world, the man who creates personal interest, is the man who gets ahead. Be liked and you will never want.

Arthur Miller

This administration is not sympathetic to corporations, it is indentured to corporations.

Ralph Nader

Method goes far to prevent Trouble in Business: For it makes the Task easy, hinders Confusion, saves abundance of Time, and instructs those that have Business depending, both what to do and what to hope.

William Penn

It is only by not paying one's bills that one can hope to live in the memory of the commercial classes.

Oscar Wilde

Capitalism

In arguing that capitalism as such is not the cause of war, I must not be taken as arguing that capitalists do not often believe in war. Believe that they and their country benefit from it.

Norman Angell

The dynamo of our economic system is self-interest which may range from mere greed to admirable types of self-expression.

Felix Frankfurter

Capitalism

It is probably true that business corrupts everything it touches. It corrupts politics, sports, literature, art, labor unions and so on. But business also corrupts and undermines monolithic totalitarianism. Capitalism is at its liberating best in a noncapitalist environment.

Eric Hoffer

What we mean when we say we are for or against capitalism is that we like or dislike a certain civilization or scheme of life.

Joseph Alois Schumpeter

You have to choose (as a voter) between trusting to the natural stability of gold and the natural stability of the honesty and intelligence of the members of the Government. And, with due respect for these gentlemen, I advise you, as long as the Capitalist system lasts, to vote for gold.

George Bernard Shaw

Censorship

Only the suppressed word is dangerous.

Ludwig Börne

Books won't stay banned. They won't burn. Ideas won't go to jail. In the long run of history, the censor and the inquisitor have always lost.

A. Whitney Griswold

...none of us would trade freedom of expression and of ideas for the narrowness of the public censor.

Hubert H. Humphrey

I thought the work would be very innocent, and one which might be confided to the reason of any man; not likely to be much read if let alone, but, if persecuted, it will be generally read.

Thomas Jefferson

Censorship reflects a society's lack of confidence in itself. It is a hallmark of an authoritarian regime.

Potter Stewart

Chance

There is no such thing as chance or accident, the words merely signify our ignorance of some real and immediate cause.

Adam Clarke

Great things spring from casualties.

Disraeli

Chance is the pseudonym of God when he did not want to sign.

Th'eophile Gautier

In the fields of observation chance favors only those minds which are prepared.

Louis Pasteur

Chance is a word void of sense; nothing can exist without a cause.

Voltaire

Change

When it in not *necessary* to change, it is necessary *not* to change.

Lucius Cary, Viscount Falkland

Change

In a progressive country change is constant; ...change ...is inevitable.

Disraeli

Change is an easy panacea. It takes character to stay in one place and be happy there.

Elizabeth Clarke Dunn

Most of the change we think we see in life is due to truths being in and out of favor.

Robert Frost

There is a certain relief in change, even though it be from bad to worse! As I have often found in travelling in a stagecoach, that it is often a comfort to shift one's position, and be bruised in a new place.

Washington Irving

Few will have the greatness to bend history itself; but each of us can work to change a small portion of events, and in the total of all those acts will be written the history of this generation.

Robert F. Kennedy

There is no sin punished more implacably by nature than the sin of resistance to change.

Anne Morrow Lindbergh

It isn't so much that hard times are coming; the change observed is mostly soft times going.

Groucho Marx

Everything changes continually. What is history, indeed, but a record of change. And if there had been very few changes in the past, there would have been little of history to write.

Jawaharlal Nehru

Change alone is eternal, perpetual, immortal.
Attributed to Arthur Schopenhauer

The older order changeth, yielding place to new,
And God fulfils himself in many ways,
Lest one good custom should corrupt the world.
Alfred, Lord Tennyson

He who rejects change is the architect of decay. The only human institution which rejects progress is the cemetery.

Harold Wilson

Character

A man's character is the reality of himself. His reputation is the opinion others have formed of him. Character is in him; reputation is from other people—that is the substance, this is the shadow.
Henry Ward Beech

In each human heart are a tiger, a pig, an ass, and a nightingale; diversity of character is due to their unequal activity.
Ambrose Gwinnett Bierce

Of all the properties which belong to honorable men, not one is so highly prized as that of character.
Henry Clay

Don't *say* things. What you *are* stands over you the while, and thunders so that I cannot hear what you say to the contrary.

Ralph Waldo Emerson

Character

Characters do not change. Opinions alter, but characters are only developed.

Disraeli

A man of character will make himself worthy of any position he is given.

Mahatma Gandhi

Character is what you are in the dark.

Attributed to Dwight L. Moody

Weakness of character is the only defect which cannot be amended.

duc François de La Rochefoucauld

A sound body is a first-class thing; a sound mind is an even better thing; but the thing that counts for most in the individual as in the nation, is character, the sum of those qualities which make a man a good man and a woman a good woman.

Theodore Roosevelt

The shortest and surest way to live with honor in the world, is to be in reality what we would appear to be; all human virtues increase and strengthen themselves by the practice and experience of them.

Socrates

An aristocrat in morals as in mind.

Owen Wister

Children

It is a great happiness to see our children rising round us, but from that good fortune spring the bitterest woes of man.

Aeschylus

You cannot teach a child to take care of himself unless you will let him try to take care of himself. He will make mistakes; and out of these mistakes will come his wisdom.

Henry Ward Beecher

Cornelia kept her in talk till her children came from school, "And these," said she, "are my jewels."

Robert Burton

Perhaps we cannot prevent this world from being a world in which children are tortured. But we can reduce the number of tortured children.

Albert Camus

I have often thought what a melancholy world this would be without children; and what an inhuman world, without the aged.

Samuel Taylor Coleridge

When children sound silly, you will always find that it is in imitation of their elders.

Ernest Dimnet

Respect the child. Be not too much his parent. Trespass not on his solitude.

Ralph Waldo Emerson

To a father waxing old nothing is dearer than a daughter. Sons have spirits of higher pitch, but less inclined to sweet, endearing fondness.

Euripides

An undutiful Daughter will prove an unmanageable Wife.

Benjamin Franklin

It is dangerous to confuse children with angels.

David Patrick Maxwell Fyfe

Children

In praising or loving a child, we love and praise not
that which is, but that which we hope for.

Johann Wolfgang Von Goethe

One father is enough to governe one hundred sons,
but not a hundred sons one father.

George Herbert

It is a wise child that knows his own father.

Homer

Give us the child for 8 years and it will be a Bolshevik
forever.

Attributed to Vladimir Ilich Lenin

Children generally hate to be idle. All the care then
should be, that their busy humor should be constantly employed in something that is of use to them.

John Locke

Children have more need of models than of critics.

Joseph Joubert

Between the dark and the daylight,
When the night is beginning to lower,
Comes a pause in the day's occupations
That is known as the children's hour.

Henry Wadsworth Longfellow

Suffer the little children to come unto me, and forbid
them not; for such is the kingdom of God.

Mark 10:14; Luke 18:16

It were better for him that a millstone were hanged
about his neck, and he cast into the sea, than that he
should offend one of these little ones.

Luke 17:2

Children

Out of the mouths of babes and sucklings hast thou ordained strength.

Psalms 8:2

A wise son maketh a glad father.

Proverbs 10:1

Even a child is known by his doings.

Proverbs 20:11

The wildest colts make the best horses.

Plutarch

Behold the child, by nature's kindly law,
Pleased with a rattle, tickled with a straw.

Alexander Pope

Lacking all sense of right and wrong, a child can do nothing which is morally evil, or which merits either punishment or reproof.

Jean-Jacques Rousseau

At first the infant,
Mewling and puking in the nurse's arms.
And then the whining school-boy, with his satchel,
And shining morning face, creeping like snail
Unwillingly to school.

Shakespeare

The children now love luxury; they have bad manners, contempt for authority; they show disrespect for elders and love chatter in place of exercise. Children are now tyrants, not the servants of their households. They no longer rise when elders enter the room. They contradict their parents, chatter before company, gobble up dainties at the table, cross their legs, and tyrannize their teachers.

Attributed to Socrates

Children

I do not love him because he is good, but because he is my little child.

Rabindranath Tagore

A child tells in the street what its father and mother say at home.

The Talmud

I have found the best way to give advice to your children is to find out what they want and then advise them to do it.

Harry S. Truman

A babe in a house is a well-spring of pleasure.

Martin Farquhar Tupper

Children begin by loving their parents. After a time they judge them. Rarely, if ever, do they forgive them.

Oscar Wilde

Heaven lies about us in our infancy.

William Wordsworth

The child is father of the man.

William Wordsworth

Give me a child for the first seven years, and you may do what you like with him afterwards.

Anonymous

Christianity

The distinction between Christianity and all other systems of religion consists largely in this, that in these others men are found seeking after God, while Christianity is God seeking after men.

Thomas Arnold

There was never law, or sect, or opinion did so much magnify goodness, as the Christian religion doth.

Francis Bacon

Let any of those who renounce Christianity. write fairly down in a book all the absurdities they believe instead of it, and they will find it requires more faith to reject Christianity than to embrace it.

Charles Caleb Colton

As to Jesus of Nazareth, my opinion of whom you particularly desire, I think the system of morals and his religion, as he left them to us, is the best the world ever saw, or is likely to see.

Benjamin Franklin

This is all the Inheritance I can give to my dear Family. The Religion of Christ can give them one which will make them rich indeed.

Patrick Henry

Had the doctrines of Jesus been preached always as pure as they came from his lips, the whole civilized world would now have been Christians.

Thomas Jefferson

Cities

When several villages are united in a single complete community, large enough to be nearly or quite self-sufficing, the state comes into existence, originating in the bare needs of life, and continuing in existence for the sake of a good life.

Aristotle

Cities

[Solon] being asked, namely, what city was best to live in, "That city," he replied, "in which those who are not wronged, no less than those who are wronged, exert themselves to punish the wrongdoers."

Plutarch

We cannot afford merely to sit down and deplore the evils of city life as inevitable, when cities are constantly growing, both absolutely and relatively. We must set ourselves vigorously about the task of improving them; and this task is now well begun.

Theodore Roosevelt

Cities are the abyss of the human species.

Jean Jacques Rousseau

Citizenship

Citizenship is no light trifle to be jeopardized any moment Congress decides to do so under the name of one of its general or implied grants of power.

Justice Hugo L. Black

The most important office, ... that of private citizen.

Louis Dembitz Brandeis

Every man among us is more fit to meet the duties and responsibilities of citizenship because of the perils over which, in the past, the nation has triumphed; because of the blood and sweat and tears, the labor and the anguish, through which, in the days that have gone, our forefathers moved on to triumph.

Theodore Roosevelt

A citizen, first in war, first in peace, and first in the hearts of his countrymen.

General Henry "Light-Horse Harry" Lee

Socrates ... said he was not an Athenian or a Greek, but a citizen of the world.

Plutarch

Good roads, good schools and good churches are a sure sign of the best citizenship produced by a free republic. How about our roads?

Author Unknown

Civilization

In civilization no man can have wholly to or for himself, and whoever would achieve power, influence, or success must cater to the tastes and whims of those who have the granting of these things in their hands.

James Truslow Adams

Civilization degrades the many to exalt the few.

Bronson Alcott

Civilization is a constant quest for nonviolent means of solving conflicts; it is a common quest for peace.

Max Ascoli

But the greatest menace to our civilization today is the conflict between giant organized systems of self-righteousness—each system only too delighted to find that the other is wicked—each only too glad that the sins give it the pretext for still deeper hatred and animosity.

Herbert Butterfield

Civilization

Civilization will not last, freedom will not survive, peace will not be kept, unless a very large majority of mankind unite together to defend them and show themselves possessed of a constabulary power before which barbaric and atavistic forces will stand in awe.

Winston Churchill

Increased means and leisure are the two civilizers of man.

Disraeli

A sufficient and sure method of civilization is the influence of good women.

Ralph Waldo Emerson

The true test of civilization is not the census, nor the size of cities, nor the crops, —no, but the kind of man the country turns out.

Ralph Waldo Emerson

No one is so savage that he cannot become civilized, if he will lend a patient ear to culture.

Horace

The greatest danger to a civilized nation is the man who has no stake in it, and nothing to lose by rejecting all that civilization stands for.

Henry Ford II

Civilization, in the real sense of the term, consists not in the multiplication, but in the deliberate and voluntary reduction of wants.

Mahatma Gandhi

We must remember that any oppression, any injustice, any hatred, is a wedge designed to attack our civilization.

Franklin D. Roosevelt

Things have their day, and their beauties in that day. It would be preposterous to expect any one civilization to last forever.

George Santayana

A civilization which develops only on its material side, and not in corresponding measure on its mental and spiritual side, is like a vessel with a defective steering gear...

Albert Schweitzer

...the nature of the breakdowns of civilizations can be summed up in three points: a failure of creative power in the minority, an answering withdrawal of mimesis on the part of the majority, and a consequent loss of social unity in the society as a whole.

Arnold J. Toynbee

The sum of the whole matter is this, that our civilization cannot survive materially unless it be redeemed spiritually.

Woodrow Wilson

Clarity

"It's very strange," said Mr. Dick . . . "that I never can get that quite right; I never can make that perfectly clear."

Charles Dickens

Clearly spoken, Mr. Fogg; you explain English by Greek.

Benjamin Franklin

I fear explanations explanatory of things explained.

Abraham Lincoln

Clarity

That must be wonderful; I have no idea of what it means.

Molière

I didn't say that I didn't say it. I said that I didn't say that I said it. I want to make that very clear.

Attributed to George Romney

Committees

A committee is a group of the unwilling, chosen from the unfit, to do the unnecessary.

Author unknown

Common Sense

If a man can have only one kind of sense, let him have common sense. If he has that and uncommon sense too, he is not far from genius.

Henry Ward Beecher

Common sense is only a modification of talent. Genius is an exaltation of it.

Edward Bulwer-Lytton

If common sense has not the brilliancy of the sun, it has the fixity of the stars.

Fernan Caballero

Common sense is, of all kinds, the most uncommon. It implies good judgment, sound discretion, and true and practical wisdom applied to common life.

Tryon Edwards

Nothing astonishes men so much as common sense and plain dealing.

Ralph Waldo Emerson

Where sense is wanting, everything is wanting.
Benjamin Franklin

The crown of all faculties is common sense. It is not enough to do the right thing, it must be done at the right time and place. Talent knows what to do; tact knows when and how to do it.
William Matthews

Common sense is the knack of seeing things as they are, and doing things as they ought to be done.
Calvin Ellis Stowe

Common sense is not so common.
Voltaire

Communism

What is a communist?—One who has yearnings for equal division of unequal earnings. Idler or bungler, he is willing to fork out his penny and pocket your shilling.
Ebenezer Elliott

The evil of communism is not its doctrinal content, which at worst is utopian, but its fanatical certainty of itself, its messianic zeal and its brutal intolerance of dissent.
James William Fulbright

They say that the Soviet delegates smile. That smile is genuine. It is not artificial. We wish to live in peace, tranquility. But if anyone believes that our smiles involve abandonment of the teaching of Marx, Engels and Lenin he deceives himself poorly. Those who wait for that must wait until a shrimp learns to whistle.
Nikita S. Khrushchev

Communism

I do not believe in communism any more than you do but there is nothing wrong with the Communists in this country; several of the best friends I have got are Communists.

Franklin D. Roosevelt

People are very much wrought up about the Communist bugaboo.

Harry S Truman

Compensation

For every thing you have missed, you have gained something else; and for every thing you gain, you lose something.

Ralph Waldo Emerson

For all our works a recompense is sure:
'Tis sweet to think on what was hard t'endure.

Robert Herrick

Give unto them beauty for ashes, the oil of joy for mourning, the garment of praise for the spirit of heaviness.

Isaiah 61:3

It is a comfort that the medal has two sides. There is much vice and misery in the world, I know; but more virtue and happiness, I believe.

Thomas Jefferson

There is no evil without its compensation. Avarice promises money; luxury, pleasure; ambition, a purple robe.

Seneca

Whoever tries for great objects must suffer something.
Plutarch

Compromise

Compromise used to mean that half a loaf was better than no bread. Among modern statesmen it really seems to mean that half a loaf is better than a whole loaf.

G. K. Chesterton

An appeaser is one who feeds a crocodile hoping it will eat him last.

Winston Churchill

If you are not very clever, you should be conciliatory.

Disraeli

...truth is the glue that holds government together. Compromise is the oil that makes governments go.

Gerald R. Ford

There isn't such a reasonable fellow in the world, to hear him talk. He never wants anything but what's right and fair; only when you come to settle what's right and fair, it's everything he wants, and nothing that you want. And that's his idea of a compromise.

Thomas Hughes

If you can't lick 'em, jine 'em.

Attributed to James E. Watson

All legislation of consequence is a series of compromises, and there are many trades and deals ... in order to get important measures through.

James E. Watson

Conference

The Conference lasted six weeks. It wasted six weeks.
It lasted as long as a Carnival, and, like a Carnival, it
was an affair of masks and mystification. Our Minis-
ters went to it as men in distressed circumstances go
to a place of amusement—to while away the time, with
a consciousness of impending failure

Disraeli

I have always said that a conference was held for one
reason only, to give everybody a chance to get sore at
everybody else. Sometimes it takes two or three conferences to scare up a war, but generally one will do
it.

Will Rogers

I originated a remark many years ago that I think has
been copied more than any little thing that I've every
said, and I used it in the *Follies of 1922.* I said America has a unique record. We *never lost a war and we
never won a conference* in our lives. I believe that we
could without any degree of egotism, single-handed
lick any nation in the world. But we can't confer with
Costa Rica and come home with our shirts on.

Will Rogers

Conformity

If you are at Rome live in the Roman style; if you are
elsewhere live as they live elsewhere.

Ambrose of Milan

These are the days when men ... seek the comfortable and the accepted; when the man of controversy is looked upon as a disturbing influence; when originality is taken to be a mark of instability; and when, in minor modification of the scriptural parable, the bland lead the bland.

John Kenneth Galbraith

Our dangers, as it seems to me, are not from the outrageous but from the conforming; not from those who rarely and under the lurid glare of obloquy upset our moral complaisance, or shock us with unaccustomed conduct, but from those, the mass of us, who take their virtues and their tastes, like their shirts and their furniture, from the limited patterns which the market offers.

Learned Hand

Fair fame is won as a rule by all who cheerfully take things as they find them and interfere with no established custom.

Philo

When people agree with me I always feel that I must be wrong.

Oscar Wilde

Congress

One of the standing jokes of Congress is that the new Congressman always spends the first week wondering how he got there and the rest of the time wondering how the other members got there.

Author unknown

Congress

No man, however strong, can serve ten years as schoolmaster, priest, or Senator, and remain fit for anything else.

Henry Adams

The rich, the well-born, and the able, acquire an influence among the people that will soon be too much for simple honesty and plain sense, in a house of representatives. The most illustrious of them must, therefore, be separated from the mass, and placed by themselves in a senate; this is, to all honest and useful intents, an ostracism.

John Adams

Too often critics seem more intent on seeking ways to alter Congress than to truly learn how it functions. They might well profit from the advice of Thomas Huxley, who said a century ago: "Sit down before facts as a little child, be prepared to give up every preconceived notion—or you shall learn nothing."

Gerald R. Ford

"Do you pray for the Senators, Dr. Hale?" someone asked the chaplain. "No, I look at the Senators and pray for the country."

Edward Everett Hale

The Senate is a place filled with goodwill and good intentions, and if the road to hell is paved with them, then it's a pretty good detour.

Hubert H. Humphrey

Congress is so strange. A man gets up to speak and says nothing. Nobody listens and then everybody disagrees.

Boris Marshalov

A jackass can kick a barn down, but it takes a carpenter to build one.

Sam Rayburn

Too many critics mistake the deliberations of the Congress for its decisions.

Sam Rayburn

And kid Congress and the Senate, don't scold em. They are just children that's never grown up. They don't like to be corrected in company. Don't send messages to em, send candy.

Will Rogers

I have come to the conclusion that one useless man is called a disgrace, that two are called a law firm, and that three or more become a congress.

Peter Stone

I think I can say, and say with pride, that we have some legislatures that bring higher prices than any in the world.

Mark Twain

It could probably be shown by facts and figures that there is no distinctly native American criminal class except Congress.

Mark Twain

Conscience

A good conscience is to the soul what health is to the body; it preserves constant ease and serenity within us, and more than countervails all the calamities and afflictions which can befall us without.

Joseph Addison

Conscience

Conscience and reputation are two things. Conscience
is due to yourself, reputation to your neighbor.

St. Augustine

What we call conscience, is, in many instances, only a
wholesome fear of the constable.

Christian Nestell Bovee

There is another man within me that's angry with me.

Thomas Browne

Conscience, good my lord,
Is but the pulse of reason.

Samuel Taylor Coleridge

The still small voice.

William Cowper

A good digestion depends upon a good conscience.

Disraeli

A good conscience is a continual Christmas.

Benjamin Franklin

The man who acts never has any conscience; no one
has any conscience but the man who thinks.

Goethe

That fierce thing
They call a conscience.

Thomas Hood

The sting of conscience, like the gnawing of a dog at a
bone, is mere foolishness.

Friedrich Nietzsche

There is no witness so terrible, no accuser so potent,
as the conscience that dwells in every man's breast.

Polybius

The worm of conscience keeps the same hours as the owl.

Schiller

The play's the thing
Wherein I'll catch the conscience of the king.

Shakespeare

We cannot live better than in seeking to become better, nor more agreeably than in having a clear conscience.

Socrates

There is no witness so terrible—no accuser so powerful as conscience which dwells within us

Sophocles

Trust that man in nothing who has not a conscience in everything.

Laurence Sterne

Conscience is, in most men, an anticipation of the opinion of others.

Henry Taylor

Conscience and cowardice are really the same thing.

Oscar Wilde

Conservation

Not one cent for scenery.

Representative Joseph G. Cannon

Conservation is ethically sound. It is rooted in our love of the land, our respect for the rights of others, our devotion to the rule of law.

Lyndon Baines Johnson

Conservation

The nation behaves well if it treats the natural re-
sources as assets which it must turn over to the next
generation increased, and not impaired, in value.
Theodore Roosevelt

Conservation and rural-life policies are really two
sides of the same policy; and down at bottom this
policy rests upon the fundamental law that neither
man nor nation can prosper unless, in dealing with
the present, thought is steadily taken for the future.
Theodore Roosevelt

Conservatives

The absurd man is one who never changes.
Auguste Barthelemy

Conservative: A statesman who is enamored of exist-
ing evils, as distinguished from the Liberal who
wishes to replace them with others.
Ambrose Bierce

A conservative government is an organized hypocrisy.
Disraeli

I am a Conservative to preserve all that is good in our
constitution, a Radical to remove all that is bad. I
seek to preserve property and to respect order, and I
equally decry the appeal to the passions of the many
or the prejudices of the few.
Disraeli

A conservative is a man who is too cowardly to fight
and too fat to run.
Elbert Hubbard

What is conservatism? Is it not adherence to the old and tried, against the new and untried'?

Abraham Lincoln

Be not the first by whom the new are tried, Nor yet the last to lay the old aside.

Alexander Pope

The man for whom the law exists—the man of forms, the Conservative, is a tame man.

Henry David Thoreau

Constancy

Without constancy there is neither love, friendship, nor virtue in the world.

Joseph Addison

A good man it is not mine to see. Could I see a man possessed of constancy, that would satisfy me.

Confucius

What is there in this vile earth that more commendeth a woman than constancy?

John Lyly

There are two sorts of constancy in love—one rises from continually discovering in the loved person new subjects for love, the other arises from our making a merit of being constant.

François de la Rochefoucauld

But I am constant as the northern star,
Of whose true-fix'd and resting quality
There is no fellow in the firmament.

Shakespeare

Constancy

There is nothing in this world constant but inconstancy.

Jonathan Swift

Constitution

I confess that there are several parts of this Constitution which I do not at present approve, but I am not sure I shall never approve them. For having lived long, I have experienced many instances of being obliged by better information, or fuller consideration, to change opinions even on important subjects, which I once thought right, but found to be otherwise.

Benjamin Franklin

The principles of a free constitution are irrecoverably lost, when the legislative power is nominated by the executive.

Edward Gibbon

The constitution, on this hypothesis, is a mere thing of wax in the hands of the judiciary, which they may twist and shape into any form they please.

Thomas Jefferson

In questions of power, then, let no more be heard of confidence in man, but bind him down from mischief by the chains of the Constitution.

Thomas Jefferson

Should the States reject this excellent Constitution, the probability is, an opportunity will never again offer to cancel another in peace—the next will be drawn in blood.

Attributed to George Washington

Contempt

Familiarity breeds contempt, while rarity wins admiration.

Apuleius

Contempt is not a thing to be despised.

Edmund Burke

The usual fortune of complaint is to excite contempt more than pity.

Samuel Johnson

Here is another man with whom I cannot get angry, because I despise him.

Benito Mussolini

Man is much more sensitive to the contempt of others than to self-contempt.

Friedrich Nietzsche

Contempt penetrates even the shell of the tortoise.

Persian Proverb

None but the contemptible are apprehensive of contempt.

François de la Rochefoucauld

Contentment

No form of society can be reasonably stable in which the majority of the people are not fairly content. People cannot be content if they feel that the foundations of their lives are wholly unstable.

James Truslow Adams

Be content with your lot; one cannot be first in everything.

Aesop

Contentment

A perverse and fretful disposition makes any state of life unhappy.

Cicero

True contentment depends not upon what we have; a tub was large enough for Diogenes, but a world was too little for Alexander.

Charles Caleb Colton

I am always content with what happens; for I know that what God chooses is better than what I choose.

Epictetus

Who is rich? He that is content. Who is that? Nobody.

Ben Franklin

You traverse the world in search of happiness, which is within the reach of every man; a contented mind confers it all.

Horace

I have learned, in whatsoever state I am, therewith to be content.

Hebrews 4:11

One should be either sad or joyful. Contentment is a warm sty for eaters and sleepers.

Eugene Gladstone O'Neill

When we cannot find contentment in ourselves it is useless to seek it elsewhere.

François de la Rochefoucauld

Discontent is the first step in the progress of a man or nation.

Oscar Wilde

Poor in abundance, famish'd at a feast.

Edward Young

Country

Every man has two countries, his own and France.
Henri De Bornier

I cannot conceive how any man can have brought himself to that pitch of presumption, to consider his country as nothing but carte blanche, upon which he may scribble whatever he pleases.
Edmund Burke

"My country, right or wrong," is a thing that no patriot would think of saying except in a desperate case. It is like saying, "My mother, drunk or sober."
G. K. Chesterton

Our country! In her intercourse with foreign nations, may she always be in the right; but our country, right or wrong.
Stephen Decatur

God grant, that not only the Love of Liberty, but a thorough Knowledge of the Rights of Man, may pervade all the Nations of the Earth, so that a Philosopher may set his Foot anywhere on its Surface, and say, "This is my Country."
Benjamin Franklin

Who saves his country, saves himself, saves all things, and all things saved do bless him! Who lets his country die, lets all things die, dies himself ignobly, and all things dying curse him!
Benjamin H. Hill

I would not change my native land
For rich Peru with all her gold
Isaac Watts

Country

For years I thought what was good for our country was good for General Motors, and vice versa. The difference did not exist.

Charles E. Wilson

Courage

Courage that grows from constitution, often forsakes a man when he has occasion for it; courage which arises from a sense of duty, acts in a uniform manner.

Joseph Addison

Often the test of courage is not to die but to live.

Vittorio Alfieri

Boldness is ever blind, for it sees not dangers and inconveniences; whence it is bad in council though good in execution.

Francis Bacon

The brave man is not he who feels no fear, for that were stupid and irrational; but he whose noble soul subdues its fear, and bravely dares the danger nature shrinks from.

Joanna Baillie

But where life is more terrible than death, it is then the truest valor to dare to live.

Thomas Browne

Courage is rightly esteemed the first of human qualities because it is the quality which guarantees all others.

Winston Churchill

Courage

Courage is that virtue which champions the cause of right.

Cicero

Every man of courage is a man of his word.

Pierre Corneille

Be scared. You can't help that. But don't be afraid. Courage from hearts and not from numbers grows.

John Dryden

Fortune befriends the bold.

John Dryden

Courage consists in equality to the problem before us.

Ralph Waldo Emerson

Courage may be taught as a child is taught to speak.

Euripides

Ain't nothing in the woods going to hurt you unless you corner it, or it smells that you are afraid. A bear or a deer, too, has got to be seared of a coward the same as a brave man has got to be.

William Faulkner

A decent boldness ever meets with friends.

Homer

Nothing is too high for the daring of mortals;
we storm Heaven itself in our folly.

Horace

What though the field be lost?
All is not lost; th'unconquerable will,
And study of revenge, immortal hate,
And courage never to submit or yield.

John Milton

Courage

The strongest, most generous, and proudest of all virtues is true courage.

Michel de Montaigne

Be of good cheer: it is I; be not afraid.

Matthew 14:27

It is better to die on your feet than to live on your knees.

La Pasionaria

I love the man that can smile in trouble, that can gather strength from distress, and grow brave by reflection. 'Tis the business of little minds to shrink; but he whose heart is firm, and whose conscience approves his conduct, will pursue his principles unto death.

Thomas Paine

We shall attack and attack until we are exhausted, and then we shall attack again.

General George S. Patton

Courage consists, not in blindly overlooking danger, but in seeing and conquering it.

Jean Paul Richter

True courage is to do, without witnesses, everything that one is capable of doing before all the world.

François de la Rochefoucauld

Far better it is to dare mighty things, to win glorious triumphs, even though checkered by failure, than to take rank with those poor spirits who neither enjoy much nor suffer much, because they live in the gray twilight that knows neither victory nor defeat.

Theodore Roosevelt

The smallest worm will turn being trodden on,
And doves will peck in safeguard of their brood.

Shakespeare

Why, courage then! What cannot be avoided
'Twere childish weakness to lament or fear.

Shakespeare

Courtesy

If a man be gracious and courteous to strangers it shows he is a citizen of the world.

Francis Bacon

Politeness. The most acceptable hypocrisy.

Ambrose Bierce

'Tis ill talking of halters in the house of a man that was hanged.

Cervantes

Politeness is the ritual of society, as prayers are of the church.

Ralph Waldo Emerson

We should be as courteous to a man as we are to a picture, which we are willing to give the advantage of the best light.

Ralph Waldo Emerson

Be civil to all; sociable to many; familiar with few.

Benjamin Franklin

To speak kindly does not hurt the tongue.

French Proverb

He was so generally civil, that nobody thanked him for it.

Samuel Johnson

Courtesy

Civility is a desire to receive it in turn, and to be accounted well bred.

François de la Rochefoucauld

Politeness costs nothing and gains everything.

Lady Mary Wortley Montagu

It is one of the greatest blessings that so many women are so full of tact. The calamity happens when a woman who has all the other riches of life just lacks that one thing.

William Osler

True politeness consists in being easy one's self, and in making every one about one as easy as one can.

Alexander Pope

Dissembling courtesy! How fine this tyrant
Can tickle where she wounds!

Shakespeare

The greater man the greater courtesy.

Tennyson

Courtship

Those marriages generally abound most with love and constancy that are preceded by a long courtship.

Joseph Addison

He that will win his dame must do
As love does when he draws his bow;
With one hand thrust the lady from,
And with the other pull her home.

Samuel Butler

Courtship to marriage is but as the music in the playhouse till the curtain's drawn.

William Congreve

If I am not worth the wooing, I am surely not worth the winning.

Henry Wadsworth Longfellow

Had we but world enough and time
This coyness, lady, were no crime.

Andrew Marvell

I will now court her in the conqueror's style;
"Come, see, and overcome."

Philip Massinger

We cannot fight for love, as men may do;
We should be woo'd and were not made to woo.

Shakespeare

The weather is usually fine when people are courting.

R. L. Stevenson

A man always chases a woman until she catches him.

Anonymous

Cowardice

Coward. One who in a perilous emergency thinks with his legs.

Ambrose Bierce

At the bottom of not a little of the bravery that appears in the world, there lurks a miserable cowardice. Men will face powder and steel because they have not the courage to face public opinion.

Edwin Hubbel Chapin

Cowardice

To see what is right and not do it is want of courage.

Confucius

The coward never on himself relies,
But to an equal for assistance flies.

George Crabbe

Many would be cowards if they had courage enough.

Thomas Fuller

Bullies are always to be found where there are cowards.

Mahatma Gandhi

Cowardice . . . is almost always simply a lack of ability
to suspend the functioning of the imagination.

Ernest Hemingway

Ever will a coward show no mercy.

Thomas Malory

It is the act of a coward to wish for death.

Ovid

The coward calls himself cautious.

Publilius Syrus

A cowardly cur barks more fiercely than it bites.

Quintus Curtius Rufus

When all the blandishments of life are gone,
The coward sneaks to death, the brave live on.

George Sewell

A coward, a most devout coward, religious in it.

Shakespeare

Cowards die many times before their deaths;
The valiant never taste of death but once.

Shakespeare

Crime

There are few better measures of the concern a society has for its individual members and its own well being than the way it handles criminals.

Ramsey Clark

The real significance of crime is its being a breach of faith with the community of mankind.

Joseph Conrad

All crime is a kind of disease and should be treated as such.

Mahatma Gandhi

The contagion of crime is like that of the plague. Criminals collected together corrupt each other They are worse than ever when, at the termination of their punishment, they return to society.

Napoleon Bonaparte

Criticism

Criticism is a disinterested endeavour to learn and propagate the best that is known and thought in the world.

Matthew Arnold

The legitimate aim of criticism is to direct attention to the excellent. The bad will dig its own grave, and the imperfect may safely be left to that final neglect from which no amount of present undeserved popularity can rescue it.

Christian Nestell Bovee

Criticism

Is it in destroying and pulling down that skill is displayed? The shallowest understanding, the rudest hand, is more than equal to that task.

Edmund Burke

As the arts advance towards their perfection, the science of criticism advances with equal pace.

Edmund Burke

Criticism is dangerous, because it wounds a man's precious pride, hurts his sense of importance, and arouses his resentment.

Dale Carnegie

It is much easier to be critical than to be correct.

Disraeli

Criticism is the art wherewith a critic tries to guess himself into a share of the artist's fame.

George Jean Nathan

Damn with faint praise, assent with civil leer
And without sneering teach the rest to sneer.

Alexander Pope

They damn what they do not understand.

Quintilian

Really to stop criticism they say one must die.

Voltaire

Critics

Let dull critics feed upon the carcasses of plays; give me the taste and the dressing.

Lord Chesterfield

Critics —murderers!

Samuel Taylor Coleridge

Those who write ill, and they who ne'er durst write,
Turn critics out of mere revenge and spite.

John Dryden

Blame where you must, be candid where you can,
And be each critic the Good-natured Man.

Oliver Goldsmith

Critic: a man who writes about things he doesn't like.

Anonymous

Curiosity

This disease of curiosity.

St. Augustine

The first and simplest emotion which we discover in
the human mind is curiosity.

Edmund Burke

Shun the inquisitive person, for he is also a talker.

Horace

Curiosity is one of the most permanent and certain
characteristics of a vigorous intellect.

Samuel Johnson

Curiosity killed the cat.

Proverb

He that pryeth into every cloud may be struck by a
thunderbolt.

John Ray

You know what a woman's curiosity is. Almost as
great as a man's!

Oscar Wilde

Curiosity

Curiosity. The reason why most of us haven't committed suicide long ago.

Anonymous

Danger

Dangers bring fears, and fears more dangers bring.
Richard Baxter

Danger, the spur of all great minds.

George Chapman

Moving of the earth brings harms and fears.
Men reckon what it did and meant.
But trepidation of the spheres
Though greater far, is innocent.

John Donne

As soon as there is life there is danger.
Ralph Waldo Emerson

Great perils have this beauty, that they bring to light the fraternity of strangers.

Victor Hugo

Out of this nettle, danger, we pluck this flower, safety.
Shakespeare

Better face a danger once than be always in fear.
Proverb

Day

Day is a snow-white Dove of heaven
That from the East glad message brings.
Thomas Bailey Aldrich

Day!
O'er nights brim, day boils at last;
Boils, pure gold, o'er the cloud–cup's brim.

Robert Browning

One day well spent is to be preferred to an eternity of error.

Cicero

He is only rich who owns the day. There is no king, rich man, fairy, or demon who possesses such power as that... The days are made on a loom whereof the warp and woof are past and future time.

Ralph Waldo Emerson

Rosy-fingered Dawn.

Homer

The day has eyes; the night has ears.

Proverb

Wait till it is night before saying it has been a fine day.

Proverb

My days are swifter than a weaver's shuttle.

Job 7:6

Listen to the Exhortation of the Dawn!
Look to this Day! For it is Life,
The very Life of Life.

Salutation of the Dawn (Sanskrit)

Night's candles are burnt out, and jocund day
Stands tiptoe on the misty mountaintops.

Shakespeare

Death

Death is a black camel, which kneels at the gates of all.

Abd-el-Kader

It is good to die before one has done anything deserving death.

Ananandrides

Men fear death as children fear to go in the dark; and as that natural fear in children is increased with tales, so is the other.

Francis Bacon

It is as natural to man to die, as to be born; and to a little infant, perhaps the one is as painful as the other.

Francis Bacon

He that unburied lies wants not his hearse,
For unto him a Tomb's the Universe.

Thomas Browne

We all labor against our own cure, for death is the cure of all diseases.

Thomas Browne

The fear of death is worse than death.

Robert Burton

Ah, surely nothing dies but something mourns!

Lord Byron

Death levels all things.

Claudian

Death is the liberator of him whom freedom cannot release; the physician of him whom medicine cannot cure; the comforter of him whom time cannot console.
Charles Caleb Colton

0 death, where is thy sting?
0 grave, where is thy victory?

I Corinthians 15:55

These have not the hope of death.

Dante

Death, be not proud, though some have called thee Mighty and dreadful, for thou art not so:

For those, whom thou think'st thou dost overthrow, Die not, poor Death. . .

John Donne

Dead men tell no tales.

English Proverb

There were some who said that a man at the point of death was more free than all others, because death breaks every bond, and over the dead the united world has no power.

Fénelon

Dust thou art, and unto dust shalt thou return.

Genesis 3:19

Show me the manner in which a nation or a community cares for its dead. I will measure exactly the sympathies of its people, their respect for the laws of the land, and their loyalty to high ideals.

Attributed to William E. Gladstone

Death is Nature's expert advice to get plenty of Life.

Goethe

Death

We die ourselves a little every time we kill in others something that deserved to live.

Oscar Hammling

How frighteningly few are the persons whose death would spoil our appetite and make the world seem empty.

Eric Hoffer

It is not right to glory in the slain.

Homer

'Tis after death that we measure men.

James Barron Hope

Sweet and glorious it is to die for our country.

Horace

In the democracy of the dead all men at last are equal. There is neither rank nor station nor prerogative in the republic of the grave.

John James Ingalls

Depend upon it, Sir, when a man knows he is to be hanged in a fortnight, it concentrates his mind wonderfully.

Samuel Johnson

I have been half in love with easeful death,
Call'd him soft names in many a mused rhyme.

John Keats

So now he is a legend when he would have preferred to be a man.

Jacqueline Kennedy

Wheresoever ye be, death will overtake you, although ye be in lofty towers.

The Koran

Were a star quenched on high,
For ages would its light,
Still travelling downward from the sky,
Shine on our mortal sight.
So when a great man dies,
For years beyond our ken,
The light he leaves behind him lies
Upon the paths of men.

Henry Wadsworth Longfellow

There is no death! What seems so is transition; this life of mortal breath is but a suburb of the life elysian, whose portal we call death.

Henry Wadsworth Longfellow

A man's dying is more the survivors' affair than his own.

Thomas Mann

The grave's a fine and private place,
But none, I think, do there embrace.

Andrew Marvell

Death has a thousand doors to let out life.
I shall find one.

Philip Massinger

Whom the gods love dies young.

Menander

Death is the golden key of eternity.

John Milton

I looked and beheld a pale horse: and his name that sat on him was Death.

Revelation 6:8

Death

Death seems to provide the minds of the Anglo-Saxon race with a greater fund of innocent amusement than any other single subject.

Dorothy L. Sayers

I have a rendezvous with Death
At some disputed barricade,
When Spring comes back with rustling shade
And apple-blossoms fill the air—
I have a rendezvous with Death
When Spring brings back blue days and fair.

Alan Seeger

Death is a punishment to some, to some a gift, and to many a favor.

Seneca

Nothing in his life became him like the leaving it.

Shakespeare

Imperious Caesar, dead and turn'd to clay,
Might stop a hole to keep the wind away.

Shakespeare

To die, —to sleep,
No more, and by that sleep to say we end
The heart-ache and the thousand natural shocks
That flesh is heir to . . . .

Shakespeare

Say nothing but good of the dead.

Solon

Do not go gentle into that good night,
Old age should burn and rave at close of day;
Rage, rage against the dying of the light.

Dylan Thomas

Each person is born to one possession which outvalues all the others—his last breath.

Mark Twain

Say the report is exaggerated.

Mark Twain

I saw him now going the way of all flesh.

John Webster

Our birth is nothing but our death begun,
As tapers waste the moment they take fire.

Edward Young

Debt

Live within your income, even if you have to borrow money to do so.

Josh Billings

The borrower runs in his own debt.

Ralph Waldo Emerson

Getting into debt, is getting into a tanglesome net.

Benjamin Franklin

And to preserve their independence, we must not let our rulers load us with perpetual debt. We must make our election between economy and liberty, or profusion and servitude.

Thomas Jefferson

I, however, place economy among the first and most important of republican virtues, and public debt as the greatest of the dangers to be feared.

Thomas Jefferson

Debt

Do not accustom yourself to consider debt only as an inconvenience; you will find it a calamity.

Samuel Johnson

One of the greatest disservices you can do a man is to lend him money that he can't pay back.

Jesse H. Jones

As an individual who undertakes to live by borrowing, soon finds his original means devoured by interest, and next no one left to borrow from—so must it be with a government.

Abraham Lincoln

Our national debt after all is an internal debt owed not only by the Nation but to the Nation. If our children have to pay interest on it they will pay that interest to themselves. A reasonable internal debt will not impoverish our children or put the Nation into bankruptcy.

Franklin D. Roosevelt

A small debt produces a debtor; a large one, an enemy.

Publilius Syrus

Deceit

God is not averse to deceit in a holy cause.

Aeschylus

It is a double pleasure to deceive the deceiver.

Jean de la Fontaine

We are never deceived; we deceive ourselves.

Goethe

Hateful to me as the gates of hell,
Is he, who, hiding one thing in his heart,
Utters another.

Homer

You can fool some of the people all of the time, and all of the people some of the time, but you cannot fool all of the people all of the time.

Abraham Lincoln

Listen at the keyhole and you'll hear news of yourself.

Proverb

The surest way to be deceived is to think one's self more clever than others.

Francois de la Rochefoucauld

Oh, what a tangled web we weave,
When first we practise to deceive!

Walter Scott

Sigh no more, ladies, sigh no more,

Men were deceivers ever.

Shakespeare

There are three persons you should never deceive: your physician, your confessor, and your lawyer.

Horace Walpole

Decision and Indecision

Somewhere deep down we know that in the final analysis we do decide things and that even our decisions to let someone else decide are really our decisions, however pusillanimous.

Harvey G. Cox

Decision and Indecision

The wavering mind is but a base possession.

Euripides

There is no more miserable human being than one in whom nothing is habitual but indecision.

William James

Decide not rashly. The decision made
Can never be recalled.

Henry Wadsworth Longfellow

Some problems are so complex that you have to be highly intelligent and well informed just to be unde-cided about them.

Laurence J. Peter

To be or not to be, that is the question...

Shakespeare

I am at war twixt will and will not.

Shakespeare

Quick decisions are unsafe decisions.

Sophocles

We have a choice: to plow new ground or let the weeds grow.

Attributed to Jonathan Westover

Defeat

Defeat never comes to any man until he admits it.

Josephus Daniels

But man is not made for defeat. A man can be de-stroyed but not defeated.

Ernest Hemingway

He said that he felt "like the boy that stumped his toe,—'it hurt too bad to laugh, and he was too big to cry.' "

Attributed to Abraham Lincoln

Those who are prepared to die for any cause are seldom defeated.

Jawaharlal Nehru

Defense

I do not hold that we should rearm in order to fight. I hold that we should rearm in order to parley.

Winston Churchill

A strong defense is the surest way to peace. Strength makes détente attainable. Weakness invites war, as my generation—my generation—knows from four very bitter experiences.

Gerald R. Ford

That is not to say that we can relax our readiness to defend ourselves. Our armament must be adequate to the needs, but our faith is not primarily in these machines of defense but in ourselves.

Admiral Chester W. Nimitz

If we desire to avoid insult, we must be able to repel it; if we desire to secure peace, one of the most powerful instruments of our rising prosperity, it must be known, that we are at all times ready for War.

George Washington

To be prepared for War is one of the most effectual means of preserving peace.

George Washington

Defense

A government without the power of defence; it is a solecism.

James Wilson

Democracy

There can be no democracy unless it is a dynamic democracy. When ... people cease to participate ... then all of us will wither in the darkness of decadence.

Saul David Alinsky

If liberty and equality, as is thought by some, are chiefly to be found in democracy, they will be best attained when all persons alike share in the government to the utmost.

Aristotle

The tyranny of a multitude is a multiplied tyranny.

Edmund Burke

Democracy will prevail when men believe the vote of Judas as good as that of Jesus Christ.

Attributed to Thomas Carle

You can never have a revolution in order to establish a democracy. You must have a democracy in order to have a revolution.

G. K. Chesterton

Democracy means government by the uneducated, while aristocracy means government by the badly educated.

G. K. Chesterton

Democracy

No one pretends that democracy is perfect or all-wise. Indeed, it has been said that democracy is the worst form of Government except all those other forms that have been tried from time to time.

Winston Churchill

It would be folly to argue that the people cannot make political mistakes. They can and do make grave mistakes. They know it, they pay the penalty, but compared with the mistakes which have been made by every kind of autocracy they are unimportant.

Calvin Coolidge

The tendency of democracies is, in all things, to mediocrity.

James Fenimore Cooper

The world is weary of statesmen whom democracy has degraded into politicians.

Benjamin Disraeli

Democracy is based upon the conviction that there are extraordinary possibilities in ordinary people.

Harry Emerson Fosdick

The measure of a democracy is the measure of the freedom of its humblest citizens.

John Galsworthy

Democracy is cumbersome, slow and inefficient, but in due time, the voice of the people will be heard and their latent wisdom will prevail.

Attributed to Thomas Jefferson.

We hold the view that the people come first, not the government.

John F. Kennedy

Democracy

All creatures are members of the one family of God.
The Koran

Democracy gives to every man
The right to be his own oppressor.
James Russell Lowell

Democracy is the theory that the common people know what they want, and deserve to get it good and hard.
H. L. Mencken

Our form of government does not enter into rivalry with the institutions of others. We do not copy our neighbours, but are an example to them. It is true that we are called a democracy, for the administration is in the hands of the many and not of the few.
Thucydides

Democracy is the recurrent suspicion that more than half of the people are right more than half of the time.
E. B. White

Dependence

The greatest man living may stand in need of the meanest, as much as the meanest does of him.
Thomas Fuller

Even in the common affairs of life, in love, friendship, and marriage, how little security have we when we trust our happiness in the hands of others!
William Hazlitt

No degree of knowledge attainable by man is able to set him above the want of hourly assistance.
Samuel Johnson

Independence? That's middle class blasphemy. We are all dependent on one another, every soul of us on earth.

George Bernard Shaw

Without the help of thousands of others, any one of us would die, naked and starved.

Alfred E. Smith

Dependence is a perpetual call upon humanity, and a greater incitement to tenderness and pity than any other motive whatever.

William Makepeace Thackeray

Desire

We trifle when we assign limits to our desires, since nature hath set none.

Christian Nestell Bovee

The thirst of desire is never filled, nor fully satisfied.

Cicero

He begins to die that quits his desires.

George Herbert

Naked I see the camp of those who desire nothing.

Horace

Some desire is necessary to keep life in motion; he whose real wants are supplied, must admit those of fancy.

Samuel Johnson

We live in our desires rather than in our achievements.

George Moore

Desire

Desire accomplished is sweet to the soul.

Proverbs 13:19

If wishes were horses, beggars would ride.

Scottish Proverb

Can one desire too much of a good thing?

Shakespeare

We desire most what we ought not to have.

Publilius Syrus

The fewer desires, the more peace.

Thomas Wilson

Despair

I want to be forgotten even by God.

Robert Browning

The name of the Slough was Despond.

John Bunyan

Despair is the conclusion of fools.

Benjamin Disraeli

Despair is the damp of hell, as joy is the serenity of heaven.

John Donne

Despondency is not a state of humility. On the contrary, it is the vexation and despair of a cowardly pride. . . .

Fénelon

The only refuge from despair is to project one's ego into the world.

Leo Tolstoy

When we have lost everything, including hope, life becomes a disgrace and death a duty.

Voltaire

Destiny

Destiny is not a matter of chance, it is a matter of choice; it is not a thing to be waited for, it is a thing to be achieved.

William Jennings Bryan

Death and life have their determined appointments; riches and honors depend upon heaven.

Confucius

Nature—pitiless in a pitiless universe—is certainly not concerned with the survival of ... any of the two billion people now inhabiting this earth. Hence, our destiny, with the aid of God, remains in our own hands.

J. William Fulbright

No man of woman born, coward or brave, can shun his destiny.

Homer

Differences

If men would consider not so much wherein they differ, as wherein they agree, there would be far less of uncharitableness and angry feeling in the world.

Joseph Addison

Even differences prove helpful, where there are tolerance, charity and truth.

Mahatma Gandhi

Differences

...if we cannot end now our differences, at least we can help make the world safe for diversity.

John F. Kennedy

Diplomacy

Diplomacy, the patriotic art of lying for one's country.

Ambrose Bierce

The first duty of a wise advocate is to convince his opponents that he understands their arguments, and sympathizes with their just feelings.

Samuel Taylor Coleridge

I never refuse. I never contradict. I sometimes forget.

Benjamin Disraeli

We must meet our duty and convince the world that we are just friends and brave enemies.

Thomas Jefferson

We have no eternal allies, and we have no perpetual enemies. Our interests are eternal and perpetual, and those interests it is our duty to follow.

Lord Palmerston

Speak softly and carry a big stick; you will go far.

Theodore Roosevelt

Discretion

An indiscreet man is more hurtful than an ill–natured one; for the latter will only attack his enemies, and those he wishes ill to; the other injures indifferently both friends and foes.

Joseph Addison

A sound discretion is not so much indicated by never making a mistake, as by never repeating it.

Christian Nestell Bovee

For good and evil in our actions meet;
Wicked is not much worse than indiscreet.

John Donne

If thou art a master, be sometimes blind, if a servant, sometimes deaf.

Thomas Fuller

The better part of valour is discretion; in the which better part I have saved my life.

Shakespeare

Dissent

Freedom of speech is useless without freedom of thought.

Spiro T. Agnew

There are only two choices: A police state in which all dissent is suppressed or rigidly controlled; or a society where law is responsive to human needs.

William O. Douglas

Dissent does not include the freedom to destroy the system of law which guarantees freedom to speak, assemble and march in protest. Dissent is not anarchy.

Seymour F. Simon

Doing

It is better to light one candle than curse the darkness.

Chinese proverb

Doing

It is some time since so few have been asked to do so much for so many on so little.

Elfan B. Rees

Doing Good

But ye, brethren, be not weary in well doing. And if any man obey not our word by this epistle, note that man, and have no company with him, that he may be ashamed.

II Thessalonians 3:13–14.

[Only by] the good influence of our conduct may we bring salvation in human affairs; or like a fatal comet we may bring destruction in our train.

Attributed to Desiderius Erasmus

Do all the good you can,
By all the means you can,
In all the ways you can,
In all the places you can,
At all the times you can,
To all the people you can,
As long as ever you can.

John Wesley

Through this toilsome world, alas!
Once and only once I pass;
If a kindness I may show,
If a good deed I may do
To a suffering fellow man,
Let me do it while I can.
No delay, for it is plain
I shall not pass this way again.

Author unknown

Doomsday

Due to the lack of experienced trumpeters, the end of the world has been postponed.

Author unknown.

The world must be coming to an end. Children no longer obey their parents and every man wants to write a book.

Attributed to an Assyrian stone tablet of about 2800 b.c.

Doubt

In contemplation, if a man begins with certainties he shall end in doubts; but if he be content to begin with doubts, he shall end in certainties.

Francis Bacon

Doubt whom you will, but never doubt yourself.

Christian Nestell Bovee

Doubting charms me not less than knowledge.

Dante

Just think of the tragedy of teaching children not to doubt.

Clarence Darrow

The doubter's dissatisfaction with his doubt is as great and widespread as the doubt itself.

Jan De Witt

Scepticism is the first step on the road to philosophy.

Denis Diderot

To have doubted one's own first principles, is the mark of a civilized man.

Oliver Wendell Holmes

Doubt

To believe with certainty we must begin with doubting.

Stanislaus Lescynski

I respect faith, but doubt is what gets you an education.

Wilson Mizner

Our doubts are traitors
And make us lose the good we oft might win
By fearing to attempt.

Shakespeare

We know accurately only when we know little; with knowledge doubt increases.

Johann Wolfgang von Goethe

Doubt makes the mountain which faith can move.

Anonymous

Dreams

As dreams are the fancies of those that sleep, so fancies are but the dreams of those awake.

Thomas Pope Blount

They are not long, the days of wine and roses:
Out of a misty dream
Our path emerges for a while, then closes
Within a dream.

Ernest Dowson

There are those, I know, who will reply that the liberation of humanity, the freedom of man and mind, is nothing but a dream. They are right. It is. It is the American Dream.

Archibald Macleish

A lost but happy dream may shed its light upon our waking hours, and the whole day may be infected with the gloom of a dreary or sorrowful one; yet of neither may we be able to recover a trace.

Walter John de la Mare

The more a man dreams, the less he believes.

H. L. Mencken

Dreams are the true interpreters of our inclinations, but art is required to sort and understand them.

Michel de Montaigne

Your old men shall dream dreams, your young men shall see visions.

Joel 2:28

Those dreams are true which we have in the morning, as the lamp begins to flicker.

Ovid

All that we see or seem
Is but a dream within a dream.

Edgar Allan Poe

The republic is a dream
Nothing happens unless first a dream.

Carl Sandburg

To sleep; perchance to dream: ay, there's the rub;
For in that sleep of death what dreams may come,
When we have shuffled off this mortal coil
Must give us pause.

Shakespeare

We are such stuff
As dreams are made on, and our little life
Is rounded out with a sleep.

Shakespeare

Dreams

You see things; and you say "Why?" But I dream things that never were; and I say "Why not?"

George Bernard Shaw

We rest.
A dream has power to poison sleep;
We rise.
One wandering thought pollutes the day.

Percy B. Shelley

If you have built castles in the air, your work need not be lost, there is where they should be. Now put foundations under them.

Henry David Thoreau

But I, being poor, have only my dreams;
I have spread my dreams under your feet;
Tread softly, for you tread on my dreams.

William Butler Yeats

Duty

In doing what we ought we deserve no praise, because it is our duty.

St. Augustine

To what gulfs a single deviation from the path of human duties leads!

Lord Byron

Men do less than they ought, unless they do all that they can.

Thomas Carlyle

The fulfilment of spiritual duty in our daily life is vital to our survival.

Winston Churchill

Do your duty and leave the rest to heaven.

Pierre Corneille

Think ever that you are born to perform great duties.

Benjamin Disraeli

The reward of one duty is the power to fill another.

George Eliot

So nigh is grandeur to our dust,
  so near is God to man,
when duty whispers low, "Thou must,"
  the youth replies, "I can."

Ralph Waldo Emerson

No personal consideration should stand in the way of performing a public duty.

Ulysses S. Grant

When occasions present themselves, in which the interests of the people are at variance with their inclinations, it is the duty of the persons whom they have appointed to be the guardians of those interests, to withstand the temporary delusion, in order to give them time and opportunity for more cool and sedate reflection.

Alexander Hamilton

Duty, then is the sublimest word in our language. Do your duty in all things . . . You cannot do more, you should never wish to do less.

Attributed to Robert E. Lee

Fear God, and keep his commandments; for this is the whole duty of man.

Ecclesiastes 12:13

We all know our duty better than we discharge it.

John Randolph of Roanoke

Duty

Majesty: when a stupid man is doing something he is ashamed of, he always declares that it is his duty.

George Bernard Shaw

There is no duty we so much underrate as the duty of being happy.

Robert Louis Stevenson

He who eats the fruit should at least plant the seed.

Henry David Thoreau

Duty is what one expects from others.

Oscar Wilde

Economy

If people starve what are they to do? Judges and magistrates wax eloquent about the increase of crime; but are blind to the obvious economic causes of it.

Jawaharlal Nehru

Too often in recent history liberal governments have been wrecked on rocks of loose fiscal policy.

Franklin D. Roosevelt

The life and spirit of the American economy is progress and expansion.

Harry S. Truman

Education

When you don't have an education, you've got to use your brains.

Anonymous

The educated differ from the uneducated as much as the living from the dead.

Attributed to Aristotle

The aim of education should be to teach us rather how to think, than what to think...

James Beattie

Education is the cheap defence of nations.

Attributed to Edmund Burke

Upon the education of the people of this country the fate of this country depends.

Benjamin Disraeli

An education isn't how much you have committed to memory, or even how much you know. It's being able to differentiate between what you do know and what you don't. It's knowing where to go to find out what you need to know; and it's knowing how to use the information you get.

Attributed to William Feather

Enlighten the people generally, and tyranny and oppressions of body and mind will vanish like evil spirits at the dawn of day.

Thomas Jefferson

If you plan for a year, plant a seed. If for ten years, plant a tree. If for a hundred years, teach the people. When you sow a seed once, you will reap a single harvest. When you teach the people, you will reap a hundred harvests.

Kuan Chung

Learned Institutions ought to be favorite objects with every free people. They throw that light over the public mind which is the best security against crafty & dangerous encroachments on the public liberty.

James Madison

Education

What spectacle can be more edifying or more season-able, than that of Liberty & Learning, each leaning on the other for their mutual & surest support?

James Madison

Education, then, beyond all other devices of human origin, is the great equalizer of the conditions of men,—the balance–wheel of the social machinery.

Horace Mann

I have never let my schooling interfere with my education.

Mark Twain

Effort

The mode by which the inevitable comes to pass is effort.

Oliver Wendell Holmes

Our spirit of enjoyment was stronger than our spirit of sacrifice. We wanted to have more than we wanted to give. We tried to spare effort, and met disaster.

Marshal Henri Petain

...I have not done as well as I should like to have done, but I have done my best, frankly and forth-rightly; no man can do more, and you are entitled to no less.

Adlai E. Stevenson

Egotism

Self–conceit may lead to self–destruction.

Aesop

Egotism

Why should I be angry with a man, for loving himself better than me?

Francis Bacon

Conceit is God's gift to little men.

Bruce Barton

I've never had any pity for conceited people, because I think they carry their comfort about with them.

George Eliot

We reproach people for talking about themselves; but it is the subject they treat best.

Anatole France

Every bird loves to hear himself sing.

German proverb

Who loves himself need fear no rival.

Latin proverb

There is not enough love and goodness in the world to throw any of it away on conceited people.

Friedrich Nietzsche

If you love yourself over much, nobody else will love you at all.

Proverb

We would rather speak ill of ourselves than not talk of ourselves at all.

Francois de la Rochefoucauld

Conceit may puff a man up, but never prop him up.

John Ruskin

Self–love, in nature rooted fast,
Attends us first, and leaves us last.

Jonathan Swift

Egotism

We are interested in others when they are interested in us.

Publilius Syrus

From his cradle to his grave a man never does a single thing which has any first and foremost object save one—to secure peace of mind, spiritual comfort, for himself.

Mark Twain

All men think all men mortal but themselves.

Edward Young

Elections

An election is coming. Universal peace is declared, and the foxes have a sincere interest in prolonging the lives of the poultry.

George Eliot

I know nothing grander, better exercise, better digestion, more positive proof of the past, the triumphant result of faith in human kind, than a well-contested ... election.

Walt Whitman

Enemies

The fine and noble way to destroy a foe, is not to kill him; with kindness you may so change him that he shall cease to be so; then he's slain.

Charles Aleyn

Rejoice not over thy greatest enemy being dead, but remember that we die all.

Apocrypha: Ecclesiasticus

Enemies

Wise men learn much from their enemies.

Aristophanes

Every man is his own greatest enemy, and as it were his own executioner.

Thomas Browne

You shall judge a man by his foes as well as by his friends.

Joseph Conrad

Some men are more beholden to their bitterest enemies than to friends who appear to be sweetness itself. The former frequently tell the truth, but the latter never.

Cato the Elder

...the common enemies of man: tyranny, poverty, disease and war itself.

John F. Kennedy

A man's foes shall be they of his own household.

Matthew 10:36

Love your enemies, bless them that curse you, do good to them that hate you...

Matthew 5:44

We have met the enemy and they are ours—

Oliver Hazard Perry

Though thy enemy seems a mouse, yet watch him like a lion.

Proverb

One enemy can do more hurt than ten friends can do good.

Jonathan Swift

Enemies

He makes no friend who never made a foe.

Tennyson

To mortify and even to injure an opponent, reproach him with the very defect or vice ... you feel ... in yourself.

Ivan Turgenev

A man cannot be too careful in the choice of his enemies.

Oscar Wilde

England

I have not become the King's First Minister in order to preside over the liquidation of the British Empire.

Winston Churchill

The late M. Venizelos observed that in all her wars England—he should have said Britain, of course—always wins one battle—the last.

Winston Churchill

[Britons] would rather take the risk of civilizing communism than being kicked around by the unlettered pot–bellied money magnates of the United States.

Tom O'brien

English Language

This is the sort of pedantry up with which I will not put.

Winston Churchill

England and America are two countries separated by the same language.

Attributed to George Bernard Shaw

The difference between the almost right word and the right word is really a large matter—'tis the difference between the lightning–bug and the lightning.

Mark Twain

Environment

I've often thought that if our zoning boards could be put in charge of botanists, of zoologists and geologists, and people who know about the earth, we would have much more wisdom in such planning than we have when we leave it to the engineers.

Justice William O. Douglas

You could cover the whole world with asphalt, but sooner or later green grass would break through.

Attributed to Ilya Ehrenburg

Never before has man had such capacity to control his own environment, ... We have the power to make this the best generation of mankind in the history or the world—or to make it the last.

John F. Kennedy

Envy

Those that are not envied are never wholly happy.

Aeschylus

Envy not greatness: for thou mak'st thereby
Thyself the worse, and so the distance greater.

George Herbert

All the tyrants of Sicily never invented a worse torment than envy.

Horace

Envy

Where envying and strife is, there is confusion, and every evil work.

James 3:16

No man likes to be surpassed by those of his own level.

Livy

Since we cannot attain to greatness, let us revenge ourselves by railing at it.

Michel de Montaigne

A slowness to applaud betrays a cold temper or an envious spirit.

Hannah More

It is a nobler fate to be envied than to be pitied.

Pindar

The truest mark of being born with great qualities is being born without envy.

François de la Rochefoucauld

Equality

The only stable state is the one in which all men are equal before the law.

Aristotle

The doctrine of human equality reposes on this: that there is no man really clever who has not found that he is stupid.

Gilbert Keith Chesterton

It is a wise man who said that there is no greater inequality than the equal treatment of unequals.

Felix Frankfurter

Men are made by nature unequal. It is vain, therefore, to treat them as if they were equal.

James Anthony Froude

Though all men are made of one metal, yet they were not cast all in the same mold.

Thomas Fuller

I have no respect for the passion for equality, which seems to me merely idealizing envy.

Oliver Wendell Holmes

That all men are equal is a proposition to which at ordinary times no sane individual has ever given his assent.

Aldous Huxley

So far is it from being true that men are naturally equal, that no two people can be half an hour together but one shall acquire an evident superiority over the other.

Samuol Johnson

Equal laws protecting equal rights . . . the best guarantee of loyalty & love of country.

James Madison

All animals are equal
But some animals are more equal than others

George Orwell

The only real equality is in the cemetery.

German Proverb

There are many humorous things in the world: among them the white man's notion that he is less savage than the other savages.

Mark Twain

Equality

Nature knows no equality; its sovereign law is subordination and dependence.

Marquis de Vauvenargues

Error

There is many a slip
'Twixt the cup and the lip.

Richard Harris Barham

I can pardon everybody's mistakes except my own.

Marcus Cato

Who errs and mends, to God himself commends.

Cervantes

It is the nature of every man to err, but only the fool perseveres in error.

Cicero

The cautious seldom err.

Confucius

Errors, like straws, upon the surface flow;
He who would search for pearls must dive below.

John Dryden

Even a mistake may turn out to be the one thing necessary to a worthwhile achievement.

Henry Ford

No man's error becomes his own Law; nor obliges him to persist in it.

Thomas Hobbes

The man who makes no mistakes does not usually make anything.

Bishop W. C. Magee

To err is human, to forgive divine.

Alexander Pope

The wise course is to profit from the mistakes of others.

Terence

I fear our mistakes far more than the strategy of our enemies.

Thucydides

The progress of the rivers to the ocean is not so rapid as that of man to error.

Voltaire

Evil

Evil events from evil causes spring.

Aristophanes

He who is good is free, even if he is a slave; he who is evil is a slave, even if he is a king.

Augustine of Hippo

Better suffer a great evil than do a little one.

Henry George Bohn

Often the fear of one evil leads us into a worse.

Nicolas Boileau

The only thing necessary for the triumph of evil is for good men to do nothing.

Attributed to Edmund Burke

God bears with the wicked, but not forever.

Cervantes

Life often presents us with a choice of evils rather than of good.

Charles Caleb Colton

Evil

Evil to him who thinks evil.

Edward III

A wicked man is his own hell.

Thomas Fuller

Don't let us make imaginary evils, when you know we have so many real ones to encounter.

Oliver Goldsmith

The evil best known is the most tolerable.

Livy

Evil. That which one believes of others. It is a sin to believe evil of others, but it is seldom a mistake.

H. L. Mencken

Every one that doeth evil hateth the light.

John 3:20

I have seen the wicked in great power, and spreading himself like the green bay tree. Yet he passed away, and lo, he was not.

Isaiah 4:7

An evil life is a kind of death.

Ovid

A good End cannot *sanctifie* evil Means; nor must we ever do Evil, that Good may come of it.

William Penn

The penalty good men pay for indifference to public affairs is to be ruled by evil men.

Attributed to Plato

Fret not thyself because of evildoers ... for they shall soon be cut down like the grass, and wither as the green herb.

Psalms 37:1–2

No man is justified in doing evil on the ground of expediency.

Theodore Roosevelt

No evil can happen to a good man, either in life or after death.

Socrates

There are a thousand hacking at the branches of evil to one who is striking at the root, and it may be that he who bestows the largest amount of time and money on the needy is doing the most by his mode of life to produce that misery which he strives in vain to relieve.

Henry David Thoreau

Excellence

The Good of man is the active exercise of his soul's faculties in conformity with excellence or virtue...

Aristotle

There are three marks of a superior man: being virtuous, he is free from anxiety; being wise, he is free from perplexity; being brave, he is free from fear.

Confucius

The pursuit of excellence is less profitable than the pursuit of bigness, but it can be more satisfying.

David Ogilvy

Experience

All experience is an arch to build upon.

Henry Adams

Experience

It is costly wisdom that is bought by experience.

Roger Ascham

Thou shalt know by experience how salt the savor is of another's bread, and how sad a path it is to climb and descend another's stairs.

Dante

The finished man of the world must eat of every apple once.

Ralph Waldo Emerson

Experience keeps a dear school, but fools will learn in no other.

Benjamin Franklin

I have but one lamp by which my feet are guided; and that is the lamp of experience. I know of no way of judging the future but by the past.

Patrick Henry

We know nothing of what will happen in future, but by the analogy of experience.

Abraham Lincoln

If history repeats itself, and the unexpected always happens, how incapable must Man be of learning from experience!

George Bernard Shaw

Happy is he who gains wisdom from another's mishap.

Publilius Syrus

When I was a boy of fourteen, my father was so ignorant I could hardly stand to have the old man around. But when I got to be twenty–one, I was astonished at how much the old man had learned in seven years.

Mark Twain

Experience is the name everyone gives to his mistakes.

Oscar Wilde

Extremism

I never dared be radical when young
For fear it would make me conservative when old.

Robert Frost

Extremism in the defense of liberty is no vice.
Moderation in the pursuit of justice is no virtue.

Senator Barry Goldwater

Facts

Facts are God's arguments; we should be careful never to misunderstand or pervert them.

Tryon Edwards

Sit down before fact as a little child, be prepared to give up every preconceived notion, follow humbly wherever and to whatever abysses nature leads, or you shall learn nothing.

Thomas Henry Huxley

Facts have a cruel way of substituting themselves for fancies. There is nothing more remorseless, just as there is nothing more helpful, than truth.

William C. Redfield, Secretary of Commerce

I often wish ... that I could rid the world of the tyranny of facts. What are facts but compromises? A fact merely marks the point where we have agreed to let investigation cease.

Author unknown

Failure

We are all of us failures—at least, the best of us are.

James Matthew Barrie

A man's life is interesting primarily when he has failed —I well know. For it's a sign that he tried to surpass himself.

Georges Clemenceau

I never blame failure—there are too many complicated situations in life—but I am absolutely merciless towards lack of effort.

F. Scott Fitzgerald

One who fears failure limits his activities. Failure is only the opportunity to more intelligently begin again.

Henry Ford

Not failure, but low aim, is crime.

James Russell Lowell

I have no use for men who fail. The cause of their failure is no business of mine, but I want successful men as my associates.

John D. Rockefeller

It is hard to fail, but it is worse never to have tried to succeed.

Theodore Roosevelt

Ambition is the last refuge of the failure.

Oscar Wilde

Faith

Faith is a higher faculty than reason.

Philip James Bailey

I believe in the incomprehensibility of God.

Honoré de Balzac

Man is not naturally a cynic; he wants pitifully to believe, in himself, in his future, in his community...

Louis Bromfield

We walk by faith, not by sight.

II Corinthians 5:7

To me, faith means not worrying.

John Dewey

They can conquer who believe they can.

John Dryden

Cast thy bread upon the waters: for thou shalt find it after many days.

Ecclesiastes 11:1.

Faith is not belief. Belief is passive. Faith is active. It is vision which passes inevitably into action.

Edith Hamilton

If ye have faith as a grain of mustard seed, ye shall say unto this mountain, Remove hence to yonder place; and it shall remove: and nothing shall be impossible unto you.

Matthew 17:20

Faith may be defined briefly as an illogical belief in the occurrence of the improbable.

H. L. Mencken

Confidence imparts a wondrous inspiration to its possessor. It bears him on in security, either to meet no danger, or to find matter of glorious trial.

John Milton

Faith

The errors of faith are better than the best thoughts of unbelief.

Thomas Russell

Faith is like love; it cannot be forced.

Arthur Schopenhauer

Faith is the antiseptic of the soul.

Walt Whitman

Fame

Time has a doomsday book, on whose pages he is continually recording illustrious names. But as often as a new name is written there, an old one disappears. Only a few stand in illuminated characters never to be effaced.

Henry Wadsworth Longfellow

Scarce any Tale was sooner heard than told;
And all who told it, added something new,
And all who heard it, made Enlargements too,
In ev'ry Ear it spread, on ev'ry Tongue it grew.

Alexander Pope

Fame is the perfume of heroic deeds.

Socrates

Fate

Our hour is marked, and no one can claim a moment of life beyond what fate has predestined.

Napoleon Bonaparte

'Tis fate that flings the dice, and as she flings
Of kings makes peasants, and of peasants kings.

John Dryden

The moving finger writes; and having writ
Moves on; nor all your Piety nor Wit
Shall lure it back to cancel half a Line.

Edward Fitzgerald

Man supposes that he directs his life and governs his actions, when his existence is irretrievably under the control of destiny.

Goethe

That which God writes on thy forehead, thou wilt come to it.

The Koran

Fate leads the willing, and drags along those who hang back.

Seneca

There is a divinity that shapes our ends,
Rough–hew them how we will.

Shakespeare

Father

Diogenes struck the father when the son swore.

Robert Burton

He that has his father for judge goes safe to the trial.

Cervantes

He that honoureth his father shall have a long life.

Ecclesiasticus 3:6

One father is more than a hundred schoolmasters.

George Herbert

If a man strike his father his hand shall be cut off.

The Code of Hammurabi

Father

A wise son maketh a glad father.

Proverbs 10:1

The fundamental defect of fathers is that they want their children to be a credit to them.

Bertrand Russell

It is a wise father that knows his own child.

Shakespeare

Fault

What an absurd thing it is to pass over all the valuable parts of a man, and fix our attention on his infirmities.

Joseph Addison

The greatest of faults is to be conscious of none.

Thomas Carlyle

Men ought to be most annoyed by the sufferings which come from their own faults.

Cicero

Faults of the head are punished in this world, those of the heart in another; but as most of our vices are compound, so also is their punishment.

Charles Caleb Colton

To acknowledge our faults when we are blamed, is modesty; to discover them to one's friends, in ingenuousness, is confidence; but to proclaim them to the world, if one does not take care, is pride.

Confucius

The defects of great men are the consolation of dunces.

Isaac D'israeli

All his faults were such that one loved him still the better for them.

Oliver Goldsmith

A fault confessed is more than half amended.

John Harington

If we had no faults, we should not take so much pleasure in remarking them in others.

François de la Rochefoucauld

He who loves not the loved one's faults does not truly love.

Spanish Proverb

The fault, dear Brutus, is not in our stars,
But in ourselves, that we are underlings.

Shakespeare

Fear

No one loves the man whom he fears.

Aristotle

No passion so effectually robs the mind of all its powers of acting and reasoning as fear.

Edmund Burke

Early and provident fear is the mother of safety.

Edmund Burke

There is a courageous wisdom; there is also a false, reptile prudence, the result not of caution but of fear.

Attributed to Edmund Burke

We listen'd and look'd sideways up!
Fear at my heart, as at a cup,
My life—blood seem'd to sip.

Samuel Taylor Coleridge

Fear

O friend, never strike sail to a fear! Come into port greatly, or sail with God the seas.

Ralph Waldo Emerson

Fear always springs from ignorance.

Ralph Waldo Emerson

Fear is the parent of cruelty.

James Anthony Froude

Let us never negotiate out of fear. But let us never fear to negotiate.

John F. Kennedy

Apprehensions are greater in proportion as things are unknown.

Livy

He who fears being conquered is sure of defeat.

Napoleon Bonaparte

Fear is a feeling that is stronger than love.

Pliny the Younger

Let me assert my firm belief that the only thing we have to fear is fear itself; nameless, unreasoning, unjustified terror which paralyzes needed efforts to convert retreat into advance.

Franklin D. Roosevelt

His flight was madness; when our actions do not, Our fears do make us traitors.

Shakespeare

To him who is in fear everything rustles.

Sophocles

Nothing is so much to be feared as fear.

Henry David Thoreau

Fear follows crime, and is its punishment.

Voltaire

Fear, like pain, looks and sounds worse than it feels.

Rebecca West

Fidelity

Give me a man that is capable of a devotion to anything, rather than a cold, calculating average of all the virtues.

Bret Harte

Be thou faithful unto death.

Revelation 2:10

The fidelity of most men is merely an invention of self-love to win confidence . . . .

François de la Rochefoucauld

Fidelity bought with money is overcome by money.

Seneca

It goes far toward making a man faithful to let him understand that you think him so; and he that does but suspect I will deceive him gives me a sort of right to do it.

Seneca

To God, thy countrie, and thy friend be true.

Henry Vaughan

Finance

Let me remind you that credit is the lifeblood of business, the lifeblood of prices and jobs.

Herbert Hoover

Finance

A holding company is a thing where you hand an accomplice the goods while the policeman searches you.
Will Rogers

Flattery

The most skillful flattery is to let a person talk on, and be a listener.

Joseph Addison

A flatterer is a friend who is your inferior or pretends to be so.

Aristotle

Imitation is the sincerest flattery.

Nathaniel Cotton

'Tis hard to find a man of great estate,
That can distinguish flatterers from friends.

Horace

The art of flatterers is to take advantage of the foibles of the great, to foster their errors, and never to give advice which may annoy.

Molière

A flattering mouth worketh ruin.

Proverbs 26:28

When flatterers meet, the Devil goes to dinner.

John Ray

We sometimes think that we hate flattery, but we only hate the manner in which it is done.

François de la Rochefoucauld

But when I tell him he hates flatterers,
He says he does, being then most flattered.

Shakespeare

They do abuse the king that flatter him:
For flattery is the bellows blows up sin.

Shakespeare

Flattery is okay if you handle it right. It's like smoking
cigarettes. Quite all right, as long as you don't inhale.

Adlai Ewing Stevenson

Flowers

Ah, Sunflower, weary of time,
Who countest the steps of the sun;
Seeking after that sweet golden clime,
Where the traveller's journey is done.

William Blake

Loveliest of trees, the cherry now
Is hung with bloom along the bough,
And stands about the woodland ride
Wearing white for Eastertide.

A. E. Housman

Consider the lilies of the field, how they grow; they toil
not, neither do they spin: And yet I say unto you, that
even Solomon in all his glory was not arrayed like one
of these.

Matthew 6:28

Lilies that fester smell far worse than weeds.

Shakespeare

Folly

The folly of one man is the fortune of another.

Francis Bacon

Folly

The hours of folly are measur'd by the clock; but of wisdom, no clock can measure.

William Blake

The first degree of folly is to conceit one's self wise; the second to profess it; the third to despise counsel.

Benjamin Franklin

When lovely woman stoops to folly,
And finds too late that men betray,
What charm can soothe her melancholy?
What art can wash her guilt away?

Oliver Goldsmith

Folly consists in drawing false conclusions from just principles, by which it is distinguished from madness, which draws just conclusions from false principles.

John Locke

I enjoy vast delight in the folly of mankind; and, God be praised, that is an inexhaustible source of entertainment.

Lady Mary Wortly Montagu

Folly pursues us in every period of life. If any one appears wise, it is only because his follies are proportioned to his age and fortune.

François de la Rochefoucauld

Fools

A fool may be known by six things: anger, without cause; speech, without profit; change, without progress; inquiry, without object; putting trust in a stranger, and mistaking foes for friends.

Arabian Proverb

But I say unto you, That whosoever is angry with his brother without a cause shall be in danger of the judgment: and whosoever shall say to his brother, Raca, shall be in danger of the council: but whosoever shall say, Thou fool, shall be in danger of hell fire.

Matthew 5:22.

A fool always finds one still more foolish to admire him.

Nicolas Boileau

Young men think old men are fools, but old men know young men are fools.

George Chapman

While the percentage of fools in this country is not so large, there are still enough to fatten the swindlers...

Champ Clark

The wise man's eyes are in his head, but the fool walketh in darkness.

Ecclesiastes 2:14

I am always afraid of a fool; one cannot be sure he is not a knave.

William Hazlitt

You may fool all the people some of the time; you can even fool some of the people all the time; but you can't fool all of the people all the time.

Attributed to Abraham Lincoln

Fools rush in where angels fear to tread.

Alexander Pope

The fool doth think he is wise, but the wise man knows himself to be a fool.

Shakespeare

Fools

Give me the young man who has brains enough to make a fool of himself.

R. L. Stevenson

Let us be thankful for the fools; but for them the rest of us could not succeed.

Mark Twain

If every fool wore a crown, we'd all be kings.

Welsh Proverb

The best way in which to silence any friend of yours whom you know to be a fool is to induce him to hire a hall. Nothing chills pretense like exposure.

Woodrow Wilson

Foreign Policy

Peace, commerce, and honest friendship, with all nations—entangling alliances with none.

Thomas Jefferson

By this I mean that a political society does not live to conduct foreign policy; it would be more correct to say that it conducts foreign policy in order to live.

George F. Kennan

The purpose of foreign policy is not to provide an outlet for our own sentiments of hope or indignation; it is to shape real events in a real world.

John F. Kennedy

The only safe rule is to promise little, and faithfully to keep every promise; to 'speak softly and carry a big stick."

Theodore Roosevelt

Forgetfulness

A man must get a thing before he can forget it.
Oliver Wendell Holmes

Blessed are the forgetful; for they get the better of even their blunders.
Friedrick Nietzsche

We have all forgotten more than we remember.
Proverb

If I forget thee, O Jerusalem, let my right hand forget her cunning.
Psalms 137:5

We bury love,
Forgetfulness grows over it like grass;
That is a thing to weep for, not the dead.
Alexander Smith

Forgiveness

You may pardon much to others, nothing to yourself.
Ausonius

Those who forgive most shall be most forgiven.
Philip James Bailey

He who forgives readily only invites offense.
Pierre Corneille

It is easier to forgive an enemy than a friend.
Madame Dorothée Deluzy

May I tell you why it seems to me a good thing for us to remember wrong that has been done us? That we may forgive it.
Charles Dickens

Forgiveness

It is often easier to forgive those who have wronged us than those whom we have wronged.

Oscar Hammling

Know all and you will pardon all.

Thomas A Kempis

Father, forgive them; for they know not what they do.

Luke 23:34

We read that we ought to forgive our enemies; but we do not read that we ought to forgive our friends.

Cosimo de' Medici

To err is human; to forgive, divine.

Alexander Pope

We pardon in proportion as we love.

François de la Rochefoucauld

If the injured one could read your heart, you may be sure he would understand and pardon.

R. L. Stevenson

There is nothing so advantageous to a man than a forgiving disposition.

Terence

A woman may consent to forget and forgive, but she never will drop the habit of referring to the matter now and then.

Anonymous

Fortune

Fortune is a god and rules men's lives.

Aeschylus

All fortune is to be conquered by bearing it.

Francis Bacon

I am not now in fortune's power;
He that is down can fall no lower.

Samuel Butler

Fortune hath somewhat the nature of a woman;
if she be too much wooed, she is the farther off.

Emperor Charles V

It is fortune, not wisdom, that rules man's life.

Cicero

Every man is the architect of his own fortune.

Appius Claudius

Ill fortune seldom comes alone.

John Dryden

Fortune, that with malicious joy
Does man her slave oppress,
Proud of her office to destroy,
Is seldom pleas'd to bless.

John Dryden

Men's fortunes are on a wheel, which in its turning
suffers not the same man to prosper for ever.

Herodotus

Human life is more governed by fortune than by reason.

David Hume

Not many men have both good fortune and good
sense.

Livy

I have a wife, I have sons; all these hostages have I
given to fortune.

Lucan

Fortune

The wheel goes round and round
And some are up and some are on the down
And still the wheel goes round.

Josephine Pollard

Fear of the future is worse than one's present fortune.

Quintilian

Everyone is the architect of his own fortune.

Abbé Regnier

Fortune never seems so blind as to those upon whom she confers no favors.

François de la Rochefoucauld

Happy the man who can endure the highest and lowest fortune. He who has endured such vicissitudes with equanimity has deprived misfortune of its power.

Seneca

Fortune, that arrant whore
Ne'er turns the key to the poor.

Shakespeare

The power of fortune is confessed only by the miserable, for the happy impute all their success to prudence or merit.

Jonathan Swift

Fortune knocks at every man's door, but in a good many cases the man is in neighboring saloon and does not hear.

Mark Twain

Freedom

The cause of freedom is the cause of God.

William Lisle Bowles

A man can be free even within prison walls. Freedom is something spiritual. Whoever has once had it, can never lose it. There are some people who are never free outside a prison.

Bertold Brecht

Hereditary bondsmen! Know ye not
Who would be free themselves must strike the blow?

Lord Byron

Perfect freedom is reserved for the man who lives by his own work and in that work does what he wants to do.

Robin George Collingwood

I am as free as nature first made man.
Ere the base laws of servitude began,
When wild in woods the noble savage ran.

John Dryden

Freedom from fear and injustice and oppression will be ours only in the measure that men who value such freedom are ready to sustain its possession—

Dwight D. Eisenhower

For what avail the plough or sail,
Or land or life, if freedom fail?

Ralph Waldo Emerson

No man is free who is not master of himself.

Epictetus

...Responsibility was the price every man must pay for freedom. It was to be had on no other terms.

Edith Hamilton

The greatest Glory of a free–born People,
Is to transmit that Freedom to their Children.

William Havard

Freedom

Who then is free? The wise man who is lord over himself; Whom neither poverty nor death, nor chains alarm, strong to withstand his passions and despise honors, and who is completely finished and founded off in himself.

Horace

When we lose the right to be different, we lose the privilege to be free.

Charles Evans Hughes

A man's worst difficulties begin when he is able to do as he likes.

Thomas Henry Huxley

Every man has a right to utter what he thinks truth, and every other man has a right to knock him down for it.

Samuel Johnson

Freedom is not merely a word or an abstract theory, but the most effective instrument for advancing the welfare of man.

John F. Kennedy

The most unfree souls go west and shout of freedom. Men are freest when they are most unconscious of freedom. The shout is a rattling of chains.

D. H. Lawrence

Those who deny freedom to others deserve it not for themselves, and, under a just God cannot long retain it.

Abraham Lincoln

There is only one cure for the evils which newly acquired freedom produces, and that is more freedom.

Thomas Macaulay

The only freedom which deserves the name, is that of pursuing our own good in our own way, so long as we do not attempt to deprive others of theirs, or impede their efforts to obtain it.

John Stuart Mill

Yet we can maintain a free society only if we recognize that in a free society no one can win all the time. No one can have his own way all the time, and no one is right all the time.

Richard M. Nixon

Those who expect to reap the blessings of freedom, must, like men, undergo the fatigues of supporting it.

Thomas Paine

Is any man free except the one who can pass his life as he pleases'?

Persius

The people who settled in New England came here for religious freedom, but religious freedom to them meant freedom only for their kind of religion. . . . This attitude seems to be our attitude in many situations today.

Eleanor Roosevelt

Man is born free—and everywhere he is in irons.

Jean Jacques Rousseau

No one can be perfectly free till all are free.

Herbert Spencer

A hungry man is not a free man.

Adlai E. Stevenson

I would rather sit on a pumpkin and have it all to myself, than to be crowded on a velvet cushion.

Henry David Thoreau

Freedom

I disapprove of what you say, but I will defend to the death your right to say it.

Attributed to Voltaire

Friendship

One friend in a lifetime is much; two are many; three are hardly possible. Friendship needs a certain parallelism of life, a community of thought, a rivalry of aim.

Henry Adams

In private conversation between intimate friends the wisest men very often talk like the weakest; for, indeed, the talking with a friend is nothing else but thinking aloud.

Joseph Addison

Beast knows beast; birds of a feather flock together.

Aristotle

For no one, in our long decline,
So dusty, spiteful and divided,
Had quite such pleasant friends as mine,
Or loved them half as much as I did.

Hilaire Belloc

Friendships multiply joys and divide griefs.

Henry George Bohn

I have loved my friends as I do virtue, my soul, my God.

Thomas Browne

You can make more friends in two months by becoming interested in other people than you can in two years by trying to get other people interested in you.

Dale Carnegie

Tell me what company thou keepest, and I'll tell thee what thou art.

Cervantes

Endeavor, as much as you can, to keep company with people above you.

Lord Chesterfield

Never injure a friend, even in jest.

Cicero

Friendship often ends in love; but love in friendship, never.

Charles C. Colton

Chance makes our parents, but choice makes our friends.

Jacques DeLille

A faithful friend is a strong defense: and he that hath found such an one hath found a treasure.

Ecclesiasticus 6:14

Animals are such agreeable friends—they ask no questions, they pass no criticisms.

George Eliot

The dearest friends are separated by impassable gulfs.
Ralph Waldo Emerson

The only way to have a friend is to be one.

Ralph Waldo Emerson

Men who know the same things are not long the best company for each other.

Ralph Waldo Emerson

A friend in need is a friend indeed.

English Proverb

Friendship

In prosperity it is very easy to find a friend; in adversity, nothing is so difficult.

Epictetus

Real friends are our greatest joy and our greatest sorrow. It were almost to be wished that all true and faithful friends should expire on the same day.

Fénelon

If you have one true friend you have more than your share.

Thomas Fuller

There is no better looking–glass than an old friend.

Thomas Fuller

'Tis thus that on the choice of friends
Our good or evil name depends.

John Gay

He was a friend to man, and lived in a house by the side of the road.

Homer

Never Explain—your Friends do not need it and your Enemies will not believe you anyway.

Elbert Hubbard

I never considered a difference of opinion in politics, in religion, in philosophy, as cause for withdrawing from a friend.

Thomas Jefferson

An injured friend is the bitterest of foes.

Thomas Jefferson

I find as I grow older that I love those most whom I loved first.

Thomas Jefferson

Greater love hath no man than this, that a man lay down his life for his friends.

John 15:13

I live in the crowds of jollity, not so much to enjoy company as to shun myself.

Samuel Johnson

If my friends are one-eyed, I look at them in profile.

Joseph Joubert

In friendship, as in love, we are often more happy from the things we are ignorant of than from those we are acquainted with.

François de la Rochefoucauld

If you want to make a dangerous man your friend, let him do you a favor.

Lewis E. Lawes

The vulgar estimate friends by the advantage to be derived from them.

Ovid

It is better to be alone than in ill company.

George Pettie

Histories are more full of examples of the fidelity of dogs than of friends.

Alexander Pope

He that goeth to bed with dogs ariseth with fleas.

James Sandford

The principal task of friendship is to foster one's friends' illusions.

Arthur Schnitzler

Friendship always benefits; love sometimes injures.

Seneca

Friendship

To lose a friend is the greatest of all evils, but endeavour rather to rejoice that you possessed him than to mourn his loss.

Seneca

Those friends thou hast, and their adoption tried,
Grapple them to thy soul with hoops of steel;
But do not dull thy palm with entertainment
Of each new–hatch'd, unfledg'd comrade.

Shakespeare

I am not of that feather to shake off
My friend when he must need me.

Shakespeare

The most I can do for my friend is simply to be his friend.

Henry David Thoreau

God save me from my friends. I can protect myself from my enemies.

Marshal de Villars

A friend is one who dislikes the same people that you dislike.

Anonymous

Future

We are always doing something for Posterity, but I would fain see Posterity do something for us.

Joseph Addison

You can never plan the future by the past.

Edmund Burke

I never think of the future. It comes soon enough.

Albert Einstein

The future is a convenient place for dreams.

Anatole France

I know of no way of judging the future but by the past.

Patrick Henry

But this *long run* is a misleading guide to current affairs. In the long run we are all dead.

John Maynard Keynes

Trust no future, howe'er pleasant!
Let the dead Past bury its dead!

Henry Wadsworth Longfellow

Take no thought for the morrow: for the morrow shall take thought for the things of itself.

Matthew 6:34

The mind that is anxious about the future is miserable.

Seneca

We know what we are, but know not what we may be.

Shakespeare

The nation is burdened with the heavy curse on those who come afterwards. The generation before us was inspired by an activism and a naive enthusiasm, which we cannot rekindle, because we confront tasks of a different kind from those which our fathers faced.

Max Weber

Gardens

Who loves a garden still his Eden keeps

Amos Bronson Alcott

Gardens

God the first garden made, and the first city Cain.
Abraham Cowley

Your sacred plants, if here below,
Only among the plants will grow.
Society is all but rude,
To this delicious solitude.

Andrew Marvell

The Lord God planted a garden eastward in Eden; and
there He put the man whom He had formed,
Old Testament: Genesis, II, 8

Many things grow in the garden that were never
sowed there.

Proverb

Generosity

True generosity is a duty as indispensably necessary
as those imposed on us by law.
Oliver Goldsmith

It is easy to become generous with other people's
property.

Latin Proverb

Genius

Doing easily what others find difficult is talent; doing
what is impossible for talent is genius.
Henri–Frederic Amiel

I have known no man of genius who had not to pay, in
some affliction or defect either physical or spiritual,
for what the gods had given him.

Max Beerbohm

Talent, lying in the understanding, is often inherited; genius, being the action of reason and imagination, rarely or never.

Samuel Taylor Coleridge

Patience is a necessary ingredient of genius.

Benjamin Disraeli

Genius must be born; it never can be taught.

John Dryden

Genius is one percent inspiration and ninety-nine percent perspiration.

Thomas A. Edison

Every man of genius sees the world at a different angle from his fellows, and there is his tragedy.

Havelock Ellis

Genius is the power of lighting one's own fire.

John Foster

A man of genius makes no mistakes. His errors are volitional and are the portals of discovery.

James Joyce

Gift, like genius, I often think only means an infinite capacity for taking pains.

Jane Ellice Hopkins

Genius is a promontory jutting out into the infinite.

Victor Hugo

Genius begets great works; labor alone finished them.

Joseph Joubert

One science only will one genius fit;
So vast is art, so narrow human wit.

Alexander Pope

Genius

The poets' scrolls will outlive the monuments of stone.
Genius survives; all else is claimed by death.

Edmund Spenser

There is a certain characteristic common to all those
whom we call geniuses. Each of them has a consciousness of being a man apart.

Miguel de Unamuno

Gifts and Giving

A man there was,
   tho' some did count him mad,
The more he cast away,
   the more he had.

John Bunyan

It is more blessed to give than to receive.

Acts 20:35

Or what man is there of you, whom if his son ask
bread, will he give him a stone?

Matthew 7:9

The most important thing in any relationship is not
what you get but what you give. . . . In any case, the
giving of love is an education in itself.

Eleanor Roosevelt

This is the law of benefits between men; the one ought
to forget at once what he has given, and the other
ought never to forget what he has received.

Seneca

You must be fit to give before you can be fit to receive.

James Stephens

I fear the Greeks, even when they bring gifts.

Vergil

God

God's mouth knows not to utter falsehood, but he will perform each word.

Aeschylus

For I would rather be a servant in the House of the Lord than to sit in the seats of the mighty.

Alben W. Barkley

There is something in the nature of things which the mind of man, which reason, which human power cannot effect, and certainly that which produces this must be better than man. What can this be but God?

Cicero

Nature herself has imprinted on the minds of all the idea of God.

Cicero

Earth with her thousand voices, praises God

Samuel Taylor Coleridge

God moves in a mysterious way
His wonders to perform.

William Cowper

Father expected a great deal of God. He didn't actually accuse God of inefficiency, but when he prayed his tone was loud and angry, like that of a dissatisfied guest in a carelessly managed hotel.

Clarence Day

God tempers the cold to the shorn lamb.

Henri Estienne

God

I have lived, Sir, a long time, and the longer I live, the more convincing proofs I see of this truth—*that God governs in the affairs of men.* And if a sparrow cannot fall to the ground without his notice, is it probable that an empire can rise without his aid?

Benjamin Franklin

God never shuts one door but he opens another.

Irish Proverb

Man proposes, but God disposes.

Thomas À Kempis

I live and love in God's peculiar light.

Michelangelo

God is our refuge and our strength, a very present help in trouble.

Psalms 16:1

The heavens declare the glory of God; and the firmament showeth his handiwork.

Psalms 19:1.

If God be for us, who can be against us?

Romans 8:31

Had I but served my God with half the zeal
I served my king, he would not in mine age
Have left me naked to mine enemies.

Shakespeare

If God didn't exist, man would have to invent Him.

Voltaire

It is the final proof of God's omnipotence that he need not exist in order to save us.

Peter de Vries

The nature of God is a circle of which the centre is everywhere and the circumference is nowhere.

Anonymous

Goodness

Goodness is easier to recognize than to define; only the greatest novelists can portray good people.

W. H. Auden

It is as hard for the good to suspect evil, as it is for the bad to suspect good.

Cicero

Good and bad men are each less so than they seem.

Samuel Taylor Coleridge

True goodness springs from a man's own heart. All men are born good.

Confucius

The good die young.

English Proverb

The ground that a good man treads is hallowed.

Goethe

He is so good that he is good for nothing.

Italian Proverb

The greatest pleasure I know is to do a good action by stealth, and to have it found out by accident.

Charles Lamb

There is no man so good, who, were he to submit all his thoughts and actions to the laws, would not deserve hanging ten times in his life.

Michel de Montaigne

Goodness

Goodness is a special kind of truth and beauty. It is truth and beauty in human behavior.
Harry Allen Overstreet

The evil that men do lives after them;
The good is oft interred with their bones.
Shakespeare

The good man is his own friend.
Sophocles

Few things are harder to put up with than the annoyance of a good example.
Mark Twain

Be good, and you will be lonesome.
Mark Twain

Government

Few consider how much we are indebted to government, because few can represent how retched mankind would be without it.
Joseph Addison

And thus Bureaucracy, the giant power wielded by pigmies, came into the world.
Honoré De Balzac

The marvel of history is the patience with which men and women submit to burdens unnecessarily laid upon them by their governments.
William E. Borah

And having looked to Government for bread, on the very first scarcity they will turn and bite the hand that fed them.
Edmund Burke

The nearest approach to immortality on earth is a government bureau.

James F. Byrnes

A thousand years scarce serve to form a state;
An hour may lay it in the dust.

Lord Byron

In the long run every Government is the exact symbol of its People, with their wisdom and unwisdom; we have to say, Like People like Government.

Thomas Carlyle

Self–government is the natural government of man.

Henry Clay

Though the people support the government, the government should not support the people.

Grover Cleveland

No man has any right to rule who is not better than the people over whom he rules.

Cyrus the Elder

...a government big enough to give you everything you want is a government big enough to take from you everything you have.

Gerald R. Ford

...it is with governments, as with religion, the form may survive the substance of the faith.

Melville W. Fuller

I can retain neither respect nor affection for a Government which has been moving from wrong to wrong in order to defend its immorality.

Mahatma Gandhi

Government

Which is the best government? That which teaches us to govern ourselves.

Johann Wolfgang Von Goethe

...that country is best governed, which is least governed ...

George Hoadly

If we can prevent the government from wasting the labors of the people, under the pretence of taking care of them, they must become happy.

Thomas Jefferson

The spirit of resistance to government is so valuable on certain occasions that I wish it to be always kept alive.

Thomas Jefferson

The legitimate object of government, is to do for a community of people, whatever they need to have done, but can not do, *at all*, or can not, *so well do*, for themselves—in their separate, and individual capacities

Abraham Lincoln

This nation, under God, shall have a new birth of freedom, that government of the people, by the people, for the people, shall not perish from the earth.

Abraham Lincoln

No man is good enough to govern another man without that other's consent.

Abraham Lincoln

That is the best government which desires to make the people happy, and knows how to make them happy.

Thomas Babington. Macaulay

We must judge of a form of government by its general tendency, not by happy accidents.
Thomas Babington Macaulay

Every country has the government it deserves.
Joseph Marie De Maistre

You have the God–given right to kick the government around—don't hesitate to do so.
Edmund S. Muskie

Men must be governed by God or they will be ruled by tyrants.
Attributed to William Penn

If men be good, government cannot be bad.
William Penn

Oligarchy: A government resting on a valuation of property, in which the rich have power and the poor man is deprived of it.
Plato

Government is like a big baby—an alimentary canal with a big appetite at one end and no sense of responsibility at the other.
Ronald Reagan

There is no credit to being a comedian, when you have the whole Government working for you. All you have to do is report the facts. I don't even have to exaggerate.
Will Rogers

Better the occasional faults of a Government that lives in a spirit of charity than the consistent omissions of a Government frozen in the ice of its own indifference.
Franklin D. Roosevelt

Government

Any government, like any family, can for a year spend a little more than it earns. But you and I know that a continuance of that habit means the poorhouse.

Franklin D. Roosevelt

The value of government to the people it serves is in direct relationship to the interest citizens themselves display in the affairs of state.

Attributed to William Scranton

It is customary in democratic countries to deplore expenditure on armaments as conflicting with the requirements of the social services. There is a tendency to forget that the most important social service that a government can do for its people is to keep them alive and free.

John Cotesworth Slessor

Whatever government is not a government of laws, is a despotism, let it be called what it may.

Daniel Webster

The world is governed more by appearances than by realities, so that it is fully as necessary to seem to know something as to know it.

Daniel Webster

My reading of history convinces me that most bad government has grown out of too much government.

John Sharp Williams

Gratitude

Earth produces nothing worse than an ungrateful man.

Ausonius

Gratitude

Next to ingratitude, the most painful thing to bear is gratitude.

Henry Ward Beecher

He who receives a benefit should never forget it; he who bestows should never remember it.

Pierre Charron

Murmur at nothing: if our ills are irreparable, it is ungrateful; if remediless, it is vain.

Charles Caleb Colton

No metaphysician ever felt the deficiency of language so much as the grateful.

Charles Caleb Colton

When I'm not thanked at all I'm thanked enough.

Henry Fielding

To the generous mind the heaviest debt is that of gratitude, when it is not in our power to repay it.

Benjamin Franklin

I will not be as those who spend the day in complaining of headache, and the night in drinking the wine that gives it.

Johann Wolfgang von Goethe

A man is very apt to complain of the ingratitude of those who have risen far above him.

Samuel Johnson

Gratitude is the least of virtues, but ingratitude the worst of vices.

Proverb

A man who is ungrateful is often less to blame than his benefactor.

François de la Rochefoucauld

Gratitude

The gratitude of most men is but a secret desire of receiving greater benefits.

François de la Rochefoucauld

Blow, blow, thou winter wind,
Thou art not so unkind
As man's ingratitude . . . .

Shakespeare

How sharper than a serpent's tooth it is
To have a thankless child.

Shakespeare

Do you like gratitude? I don't. If pity is akin to love, gratitude is akin to the other thing.

George Bernard Shaw

Alas! the gratitude of men
Hath often left me mourning.

William Wordsworth

Greatness

There are some men who lift the age they inhabit, till all men walk on higher ground in that lifetime.

Maxwell Anderson

There be three things which make a nation great and prosperous: a fertile soil, busy workshops, easy conveyance for men and goods from place to place.

Francis Bacon

Great men are the guideposts and landmarks in the state.

Edmund Burke

The price of greatness is responsibility.

Winston Churchill

Not he is great who can alter matter, but he who can alter my state of mind.

Ralph Waldo Emerson

The world cannot live at the level of its great men.

James Frazer

There aren't any great men. There are just great challenges that ordinary men like you and me are forced by circumstances to meet.

Attributed to Admiral William F. Halsey

No really great man ever thought himself so.

William Hazlitt

There would be no great ones if there were no little ones.

George Herbert

I think this is the most extraordinary collection of talent, of human knowledge, that has ever been gathered together at the White House, with the possible exception of when Thomas Jefferson dined alone.

John F. Kennedy

Great men are not always wise.

Job 32:9

Be not afraid of greatness. Some are born great, some achieve greatness, and some have greatness thrust upon them.

Shakespeare

There was never a nation great until it came to the knowledge that it had nowhere in the world to go for help.

Charles Dudley Warner

Greed

We find greedy men, blind with the lust for money, trafficking in human misery,

General Thomas C. Clark

What man calls civilization always results in deserts. Man is never on the square—he uses up the fat and greenery of the earth. Each generation wastes a little more of the future with greed and lust for riches.

Don Marquis

Grief

It is dangerous to abandon one's self to the luxury of grief: it deprives one of courage, and even of the wish for recovery.

Henri–Frederic Amiel

There is no grief which time does not lessen and soften.

Cicero

Grief is the agony of an instant: the indulgence of grief the blunder of a life.

Benjamin Disraeli

If our inward griefs were seen written on our brow, how many would be pitied who are now envied.

Metastasio

Grief is a tree that has tears for its fruit.

Philemon

Guilt

The pot calls the kettle black.

Cervantes

Guilt is present in the very hesitation, even though the deed be not committed.

Cicero

The greatest incitement to guilt is the hope of sinning with impunity.

Cicero

He who flies proves himself guilty.

Danish proverb

Secret guilt by silence is betrayed.

John Dryden

That deed which in our guilt we today call weakness, will appear tomorrow as an essential link in the complete chain of Man.

Kahlil Gibran

Men's minds are too ready to excuse guilt in themselves.

Livy

He that knows no guilt can know no fear.

Philip Massinger

The wicked flee when no man pursueth.

Proverbs 28:1.

He declares himself guilty who justifies himself before accusation.

Proverb

Whoever blushes, is already guilty; true innocence is ashamed of nothing.

Jean Jacques Rousseau

And oftentimes excusing of a fault
Doth make the fault the worse by the excuse.

Shakespeare

Guilt

The lady doth protest too much, methinks.

Shakespeare

From the body of one guilty deed a thousand ghostly fears and haunting thoughts proceed.

William Wordsworth

Habit

Habit, if not resisted, soon becomes necessity.

Augustine of Hippo

Habit is a sort of second nature.

Cicero

It seems, in fact, as though the second half of a man's life is made up of nothing but the habits he has accumulated during the first half.

Fëodor Dostoevski

The chains of habit are generally too small to be felt until they are too strong to be broken.

Samuel Johnson

Habit is a cable; we weave a thread of it every day, and at last we cannot break it.

Horace Mann

How use doth breed a habit in a man!

Shakespeare

When a man boasts of his bad habits, you may rest assured they are the best he has.

Woodrow Wilson

Hands

Living from hand to mouth, soon satisfi'd.

Guillaume Du Bartas

158

Let not thy left hand know what thy right hand doeth.
New Testament: Matthew, *VI, 3*

Many hands make light work.

Proverb

One hand washeth the other.

Seneca

All the perfumes of Arabia will not sweeten this little hand.

Shakespeare

See, how she leans her cheek upon her hand!
0, that I were a glove upon that hand,
That I might touch that cheek!

Shakespeare

His hand will be against every man and every man's hand against him.

Genesis 16:12

Happiness

Hold him alone truly fortunate who has ended his life in happy well-being.

Aeschylus

Happiness is at once the best, the noblest and the pleasantest of things.

Aristotle

No man is happy who does not think himself so.
Marcus Aurelius

Happiness sneaks in through a door you didn't know you left open.

John Barrymore

Happiness

What is given by the gods more desirable than a happy hour?

Catullus

The happiness of life is made up of minute fractions—the little soon forgotten charities of a kiss or smile, a kind look, a heartfelt compliment, and the countless infinitesimals of pleasurable and genial feeling.

Samuel Taylor Coleridge

To find out what one is fitted to do and to secure an opportunity to do it is the key to happiness.

John Dewey

Happiness makes up in height for what it lacks in length.

Robert Frost

Often the greatest enemy of present happiness is past happiness too well remembered.

Oscar Hammling

And there is even a happiness
That makes the heart afraid.

Thomas Hood

The supreme happiness of life is the conviction that we are loved.

Victor Hugo

He is happiest of whom the world says least, good or bad.

Thomas Jefferson

In order to be happy oneself it is necessary to make at least one other person happy... The secret of human happiness is not in self-seeking but in self-forgetting.

Theodore Reik

The happiness or unhappiness of men depends no less upon their dispositions than on their fortunes.

François de la Rochefoucauld

Oh, how bitter a thing it is to look into happiness through another man's eyes.

Shakespeare

Happiness is the shadow of things past,
Which fools still take for that which is to be!

Francis Thompson

The sun and stars that float in the open air;
The apple–shaped earth, and we upon it—
　　　surely the drift of them is something grand!
I do not know what it is, except that it is grand,
　　　and that it is happiness.

Walt Whitman

All the things I really like to do are either immoral, illegal, or fattening.

Attributed to Alexander Woollcott

Hatred

Hatred does not cease by hatred, but only by love; this is the eternal rule.

Buddha

Now hatred is by far the greatest pleasure;
Men love in haste, but they detest at leisure.

Lord Byron

People hate those who make them feel their own inferiority.

Lord Chesterfield

Hatred

There are glances of hatred that stab and raise no cry of murder.

George Eliot

Hating people is like burning down your own house to get rid of a rat.

Harry Emerson Fosdick

Men hate more steadily than they love.

Samuel Johnson

I could never hate anyone I knew.

Attributed to Charles Lamb

For never can true reconcilement grow,
Where wounds of deadly hate have pierced so deep.

John Milton

Whom men fear they hate, and whom they hate, they wish dead.

Quintus Ennius

There is no sport in hate when all the rage
Is on one side.

Percy B. Shelley

It is characteristic of human nature to hate the man whom you have wronged.

Tacitus

As love, if love be perfect, casts out fear,
So hate, if hate be perfect, casts out fear.

Tennyson

Health

If you want to know if your brain is flabby feel of your legs.

Bruce Barton

In nothing do men more nearly approach the gods than in giving health to men.

Cicero

The health of the people is really the foundation upon which all their happiness and all their powers as a State depend.

Benjamin Disraeli

Health is not a condition of matter, but of Mind.

Mary Baker G. Eddy

Be sober and temperate, and you will be healthy.

Benjamin Franklin

0 health! health! the blessing of the rich! the riches of the poor! who can buy thee at too dear a rate, since there is no enjoying this world without thee?

Ben Jonson

Our prayers should be for a sound mind in a healthy body.

Juvenal

Life is not merely being alive, but being well.

Martial

A man in good health is always full of advice to the sick.

Menander

It is part of the cure to wish to be cured.

Seneca

Heart

The heart has reasons that reason does not understand.

Jacques Bénigne Bossuet

Heart

Maid of Athens, ere we part,
Give, oh, give me back my heart!

Lord Byron

Faint heart never won fair lady.

William Camden

The heart of a wise man should resemble a mirror, which reflects every object without being sullied by any.

Confucius

A kind heart is a fountain of gladness, making everything in its vicinity to freshen into smiles.

Washington Irving

Let not your heart be troubled.

John 14:1

The heart has eyes that the brain knows nothing of.

Dr. Charles Henry Parkhurst

And let me wring your heart; for so I shall,
If it be made of penetrable stuff.

Shakespeare

He hath a heart as sound as a bell and his tongue is the clapper, for what his heart thinks his tongue speaks.

Shakespeare

My heart is a lonely hunter that hunts on a lonely hill.

William Sharp

Heaven

All places are distant from heaven alike.

Robert Burton

To Appreciate heaven well
'Tis good for a man to have some fifteen minutes of hell.

Will Carleton

What a man misses mostly in heaven is company.

Mark Twain

And so upon this wise I prayed,—
  Great Spirit, give to me
  A heaven not so large as yours
  But large enough for me.

Emily Dickinson

In my father's house are many mansions.

John 14:2

What came from the earth returns back to the earth, and the spirit that was sent from heaven, again carried back, is received into the temple of heaven.

Lucretius

Here we may reign secure; and in my choice
To reign is worth ambition, though in Hell:
Better to reign in Hell, than serve in Heav'n.

John Milton

Hell

Hell is full of good intentions or desires.

St. Bernard of Clairvaux

Abandon every hope, ye who enter here.

Dante

I found the original of my hell in the world which we inhabit.

Dante

Hell

Men might go to heaven with half the labor they put to go to hell, if they would but venture their industry in the right way.

Ben Jonson

Hell is a circle about the unbelieving.

The Koran

Hell hath no limits, nor is circumscrib'd
In one self–place; for where we are is hell;
And where hell is, there must we ever be;
And to conclude, when all the world dissolves,
And every creature shall be purified,
All places shall be hell that are not heaven.

Christopher Marlowe

Myself am Hell;
And, in the lowest deep, a lower deep,
Still threat'ning to devour me, opens wide;
To which the hell I suffer seems a heaven.

John Milton

Heroism

No man is a hero to his valet.

Mlle. Aisse

Heroism is the brilliant triumph of the soul over the flesh—that is to say, over fear... Heroism is the dazzling and glorious concentration of courage.

Henri–Frederic Amiel

Let us so bear ourselves that if the British Commonwealth lasts for a thousand years, men will still say, 'This was their finest hour."

Winston Churchill

Heroism feels and never reasons and therefore is always right.

Ralph Waldo Emerson

There is nothing more touching than the sight of a Nation in search of its great men, nothing more beautiful than its readiness to accept a hero on trust.

James Russell Lowell

History

The great object in trying to understand history is to get behind men and grasp ideas.

Lord Acton

Neither history nor economics can be intelligently studied without a constant reference to the geographical surroundings which have affected different nations.

Henry Adams

History gives us a kind of chart, and we dare not surrender even a small rushlight in the darkness. The hasty reformer who does not remember the past will find himself condemned to repeat it.

John Buchan

Biography is the only true history.

Thomas Carlyle

Want of foresight, unwillingness to act when action would be simple and effective, lack of clear thinking, confusion of counsel until the emergency comes, until self-preservation strikes its jarring gong—these are the features which constitute the endless repetition of history.

Winston Churchill

History

To be ignorant of what occurred before you were born is to remain always a child.

Cicero

History is the witness of the times, the torch of truth, the life of memory, the teacher of life, the messenger of antiquity.

Cicero

History is little more than the register of the crimes, follies, and misfortunes of mankind.

Edward Gibbon

All history, so far as it is not supported by contemporary evidence, is romance.

Samuel Johnson

History is clarified experience.

James Russell Lowell

Hegel remarks somewhere that all great world–historic facts and personages appear, so to speak, twice. He forgot to add: the first time as tragedy, the second time as fame.

Karl Marx

What is history but a fable agreed upon?

Napoleon Bonaparte

Human history becomes more and more a race between education and catastrophe.

H. G. Wells

Home

You are a King by your own Fireside, as much as any Monarch on his Throne.

Cervantes

In love of home, the love of country has its rise.

Charles Dickens

Home is the place where, when you have to go there,
They have to take you in.

Robert Frost

It takes a heap o' livin' in a house t' make it home.

Edgar A. Guest

It was the policy of the good old gentleman to make
his children feel that home was the happiest place in
the world; and I value this delicious home feeling as
one of the choicest gifts a parent can bestow.

Washington Irving

To be happy at home is the ultimate result of all ambition, the end to which every enterprise and labor
tends, and of which every desire prompts the prose-
cution.

Samuel Johnson

Be it ever so humble, there's no place like home.

John Howard Payne

The poorest man may in his cottage bid defiance to all
the forces of the Crown. It may be frail—its roof may
shake—the wind may blow through it—the storm may
enter—the rain may enter—but the King of England
cannot enter!—all his force dares not cross the
threshold of the ruined tenement!

William Pitt, the Elder

Home is where the heart is.

Pliny the Elder

As a bird that wandereth from her nest, so is a man
that wandereth from his place.

Proverbs 27:8

Home

When I was at home I was in a better place.

Shakespeare

Honesty

He who says there is no such thing as an honest man, is himself a knave.

George Berkeley

A trustee is held to something stricter than the morals of the market place. Not honesty alone, but the punctilio of an honor the most sensitive, is then the standard of behavior.

Benjamin N. Cardozo

Make yourself an honest man, and then you may be sure that there is one rascal less in the world.

Thomas Carlyle

Honesty is the best policy.

Cervantes

The darkest hour in the history of any young man is when he sits down to study how to get money without honestly earning it.

Horace Greeley

If he were to be made honest by an act of parliament I should not alter in my faith of him.

Ben Jonson

A man is sorry to be honest for nothing.

Ovid

An honest man is the noblest work of God.

Alexander Pope

The only disadvantage of an honest heart is credulity.

Philip Sidney

Accuracy is the twin brother of honesty; inaccuracy, of dishonesty.

Charles Simmons

Honor

Dignity consists not in possessing honors, but in the consciousness that we deserve them.

Aristotle

Honorable descent is, in all nations, greatly esteemed. It is to be expected that the children of men of worth will be like the progenitors; for nobility is the virtue of a family.

Aristotle

The best memorial for a mighty man is to gain honour ere death.

Beowulf

Our own heart, and not other men's opinion, forms our true honor.

Samuel Taylor Coleridge

It is of no consequence of what parents a man is born, so he be a man of merit.

Horace

Better a thousand times to die with glory than live without honor.

Louis VI of France

Nothing is more disgraceful than for a man who is nothing, to hold himself honored on account of his forefathers; and yet hereditary honors are a noble and splendid treasure to descendants.

Plato

Honor

Set honour in one eye and death i' the other
And I will look on both indifferently;
For let the gods so speed me as I love
The name of honour more than I fear death.

Shakespeare

Mine honour is my life; both grow in one;
Take honour from me and my life is done.

Shakespeare

The shortest and surest way to live with honor in the
world, is to be in reality what we would appear to be.

Socrates

Hope

I live on hope and that I think do all
Who come into this world.

Robert Bridges

Man is, properly speaking, based upon hope; he has
no other possession but hope; this world of his is em-
phatically the place of hope.

Thomas Carlyle

To the sick, while there is life there is hope.

Cicero

He that lives on hope will die fasting.

Benjamin Franklin

Hope is a delusion; no hand can grasp a wave or a
shadow.

Victor Marie Hugo

Hope is itself a species of happiness, and, perhaps,
the chief happiness which this world affords.

Samuel Johnson

The setting of a great hope is like the setting of the sun. The brightness of our life is gone.

Henry Wadsworth Longfellow

Hopes are but the dreams of those who wake.

Pindar

Hope springs eternal in the human breast;
Man never is, but always to be blest.

Alexander Pope

Hope, dead lives nevermore,
No, not in heaven.

Christina Rossetti

True hope is swift, and flies with swallow's wings;
Kings it makes gods, and meaner creatures kings.

Shakespeare

You believe easily that which you hope for earnestly.

Terence

We did not dare to breathe a prayer
        Or to give our anguish scope!
Something was dead in each of us,
        And what was dead was hope.

Oscar Wilde

Hospitality

When there is room in the heart there is room in the house.

Danish Proverb

Hospitality consists in a little fire, a little food, and an immense quiet.

Ralph Waldo Emerson

Hospitality

Then why should I sit in the scorner's seat,
     Or hurl the cynic's ban?
Let me live in my house by the side of the road,
     And be a friend to man.

Sam Walter Foss

Hail Guest! We ask not what thou art:
If Friend, we greet thee, hand and heart;
If Stranger, such no longer be;
If Foe, our love shall conquer thee.

Arthur Guiterman

Be not forgetful to entertain strangers, for thereby some have entertained angels unawares.

Hebrews 13:2

True friendship's laws are by this rule express'd,
Welcome the coming, speed the parting guest.

Homer

Fish and guests in three days are stale.

John Lyly

I had three chairs in my house: one for solitude, two for friendship, three for society.

Henry David Thoreau

Humility

Lowliness is the base of every virtue,
And he who goes the lowest builds the safest.

Philip J. Bailey

Humility is the solid foundation of all the virtues.

Confucius

I ate umble pie with an appetite.

Charles Dickens

After crosses and losses men grow humbler and wiser.
Benjamin Franklin

To be humble to superiors, is duty; to equals, is courtesy; to inferiors, is nobleness; and to all, safety;...

Thomas Moore

Whosoever shall smite thee on thy right cheek, turn to him the other also.
Matthew 5:39; Luke 6:29

Whosoever shall compel thee to go a mile, go with him twain.

Matthew 6:41

Hunger

Hunger is the best sauce in the world.

Cervantes

An empty stomach is not a good political adviser.
Albert Einstein

They that die by famine die by inches.

Matthew Henry

Death in all its shapes is hateful to unhappy man, but the worst is death from hunger.

Homer

If thine enemy be hungry, give him bread to eat.
Lamentations 4:9

Husband

It is necessary to be almost a genius to make a good husband.

Honoré de Balzac

Husband

We wedded men live in sorrow and care.

Geoffrey Chaucer

An archaeologist is the best husband any woman can have: the older she gets, the more interested he is in her.

Agatha Christie

Let the husband render unto the wife due benevolence: and likewise also the wife unto the husband.

I Corinthians 7:3

A husband's patience atones for all crimes.

Heinrich Heine

Idealism

No folly is more costly than the folly of intolerant idealism.

Winston Churchill

An idealist believes the short run doesn't count. A cynic believes the long run doesn't matter. A realist believes that what is done or left undone in the short run determines the long run.

Sidney J. Harris

Man is born a predestined idealist, for he is born to act. To act is to affirm the worth of an end, and to persist in affirming the worth of an end is to make an ideal.

Oliver Wendell Holmes

An idealist is one who, on noticing that a rose smells better than a cabbage, concludes that it is also more nourishing.

H. L. Mencken

Ideals are like the stars: we never reach them, but like the mariners of the sea, we chart our course by them.
Carl Schurz

Ideas

Our land is not more the recipient of the men of all countries than of their ideas.
George Bancroft

An idea, like a ghost, according to the common notion of ghosts, must be spoken to a little before it will explain itself.
Charles John Huffam Dickens

Mr. Kremlin himself was distinguished for ignorance, for he had only one idea,—and that was wrong.
Benjamin Disraeli

The key to every man is his thought... He can only be reformed by showing him a new idea which commands his own.
Ralph Waldo Emerson

The test of a first-rate intelligence is the ability to hold two opposed ideas in the mind, at the same time, and still retain the ability to function.
F. Scott Fitzgerald

The real Antichrist is he who turns the wine of an original idea into the water of mediocrity.
Eric Hoffer

Idleness

Idleness is sweet, and its consequences are cruel.
Attributed to John Quincy Adams

Idleness

Lost time is never found again.

John Hill Aughey

Idleness is only the refuge of weak minds, and the holiday of fools.

Lord Chesterfield

Absence of occupation is not rest,
A mind quite vacant is a mind distressed.

William Cowper

There is no place in civilization for the idler. None of us has any right to ease.

Henry Ford

Laziness travels so slowly that poverty soon overtakes him.

Benjamin Franklin

The way to be nothing is to do nothing.

Nathaniel Howe

To be idle and to be poor have always been reproaches, and therefore every man endeavors with his utmost care to hide his poverty from others, and his idleness from himself.

Samuel Johnson

Go to the ant, thou sluggard; consider her ways, and be wise.

Proverbs, 6:6

Of all our faults, the one that we excuse most easily is idleness.

François de la Rochefoucauld

Not only is he idle who is doing nothing, but he that might be better employed.

Socrates

For Satan finds some mischief still
For idle hands to do.

Isaac Watts

To do nothing at all is the most difficult thing in the world, the most difficult and the most intellectual.

Oscar Wilde

Ignorance

Behind every argument is someone's ignorance.

Louis Brandeis

Ignorance is the night of the mind, but a night without moon or star.

Confucius

To be conscious that you are ignorant is a great step to knowledge.

Benjamin Disraeli

To the ignorant even the words of the wise seem foolishness.

Euripides

No more; where ignorance is bliss, 'Tis folly to be wise.

Thomas Gray

Ignorance of the law excuses no man: not that all can know the law, but because 'tis an excuse everyone will plead, and no man can tell how to refute him.

John Selden

There is no darkness, but ignorance.

Shakespeare

Nothing is worse than active ignorance.

Johann Wolfgang Von Goethe

Ignorance

Everybody is ignorant only on different subjects.

Will Rogers

So oft in theologic wars,
The disputants, I ween,
Rail on in utter ignorance
Of what each other mean,
And prate about an Elephant
Not one of them has seen!

John Godfrey Saxe

Ignorant men
Don't know what good they hold in their hands until
They've flung it away.

Sophocles

Imagination

The human race is governed by its imagination.

Napoleon Bonaparte

To know is nothing at all; to imagine is everything.

Anatole France

Were it not for imagination a man would be as happy
in the arms of a chambermaid as of a duchess.

Samuel Johnson

His imagination resembled the wings of an ostrich. It
enabled him to run, though not to soar.

Thomas B. Macaulay

Imitation

Men often applaud an imitation, and hiss the real
thing.

Aesop

Was Christ a man like us?
Ah! let us try if we then, too, can be such men as he!

Matthew Arnold

Imitation is the sincerest flattery.

Charles C. Colton

He who imitates what is evil always goes beyond the example that is set; on the contrary, he who imitates what is good always falls short.

Francesco Guicciardini

When people are free to do as they please, they usually imitate each other.

Eric Hoffer

Agesilaus, being invited once to hear a man who admirably imitated the nightingale, declined, saying he had heard the nightingale itself.

Plutarch

A great part of art consists in imitation. For the whole conduct of life is based on this: that what we admire in others we want to do ourselves.

Quintilian

Immortality

Let us not lament too much the passing of our friends. They are not dead, but simply gone before us along the road which all must travel.

Antiphanes

Whatsoever that be within us that feels, thinks, desires, and animates, is something celestial, divine, and, consequently, imperishable.

Aristotle

Immortality

My humble friend, we know not how to live this life which is so short yet seek one that never ends.

Anatole France

Either the soul is immortal and we shall not die, or it perishes with the flesh, and we shall not know that we are dead. Live, then, as if you were eternal.

André Maurois

What we have done for ourselves alone dies with us; what we have done for others and the world remains and is immortal.

Attributed to Albert Pike

Independence

The moral progression of a people can scarcely begin till they are independent.

James Martineau

To be independent is the business of a few only; it is the privilege of the strong.

Friedrich Nietzsche

Individual

Be faithful to that which exists nowhere but in yourself–and thus make yourself indispensable.

Andre Gide

Whatever crushes individuality is despotism, by whatever name it may be called.

John Stuart Mi"

An individual is as superb as a nation when he has the qualities which make a superb nation.

Walt Whitman

Creative ideas do not spring from groups. They spring from individuals. The divine spark leaps from the finger of God to the finger of Adam, whether it takes ultimate shape in a law of physics or a law of the land, a poem or a policy, a sonata or a mechanical computer.

A. Whitney Griswold

I am only one,
But still I am one.
I cannot do everything,
But still I can do something;
And because I cannot do everything
I will not refuse to do the something that I can do.

Edward Everett Hale

But society has now fairly got the better of individuality; and the danger which threatens human nature is not the excess, but the deficiency, of personal impulses and preferences.

John Stuart Mill

Individuality is everywhere to be spared and respected as the root of everything good.

Jean Paul Richter

If a man does not keep pace with his companions, perhaps it is because he hears a different drummer. Let him step to the music which he hears, however measured or far away.

Henry David Thoreau

Ingratitude

People who bite the hand that feeds them usually lick the boot that kicks them.

Eric Hoffer

Ingratitude

If you pick up a starving dog and make him prosperous, he will not bite you. That is the principal difference between a dog and a man.

Mark Twain

Injustice

No one will dare maintain that it is better to do injustice than to bear it.

Aristotle

I know there is a God, and that He hates injustice and slavery. I see the storm coming, and I know that His hand is in it. If he has a place and work for me—and I think He has—I believe I am ready.

Attributed to Abraham Lincoln

He who commits injustice is ever made more wretched than he who suffers it.

Plato

If you give me six lines written by the hand of the most honest of men, I will find something in them which will hang him.

Cardinal Richelieu

He who has injured thee was either stronger or weaker than thee. If weaker, spare him; if stronger, spare thyself.

Seneca

Men's indignation, it seems, is more excited by legal wrong than by violent wrong, the first looks like being cheated by an equal, the second like being compelled by a superior.

Thucydides

Isolationism

Perfectionism, no less than isolationism or imperialism or power politics, may obstruct the paths to international peace. Let us not forget that the retreat to isolationism a quarter of a century ago was started not by a direct attack against international cooperation but against the alleged imperfections of the peace.

Franklin D. Roosevelt

I have no confidence in the system of *isolement* [isolation]. It does not answer in social life for individuals, nor in politics for nations. Man is a social animal.

Arthur Wellesley, Duke of Wellington

Jealousy

Jealousy is ... a tiger that tears not only its prey but also its own raging heart.

Michael Beer

Anger and jealousy can no more bear to lose sight of their objects than love.

George Eliot

Though jealousy be produced by love, as ashes are by fire, yet jealousy extinguishes love as ashes smother the flame.

Margaret of Navarre

O! beware, my lord, of jealousy
It is the green–eyed monster which doth mock
The meat it feeds on.

Shakespeare

Jealousy

Love is strong as death; jealousy is cruel as the grave.
Song of Solomon 8:6

Joy

Joy rises in me like a summer's morn.
Samuel Taylor Coleridge

My theory is to enjoy life, but the practice is against it.

Charles Lamb

My candle burns at both ends,
It will not last the night;
But ah, my foes, and oh, my friends,
It gives a lovely light!
Edna St. Vincent Millay

Drink and dance and laugh and lie,
Love the reeling midnight through,
For tomorrow we shall die!
(But, alas, we never do.)
Dorothy Parker

Weeping may endure for a night, but joy cometh in the morning.
Psalms 30:5

A joy that's shared is a joy made double.
John Ray

Occasionally in life there are those moments of unutterable fulfillment which cannot be completely explained by those symbols called words. Their meanings can only be articulated by the inaudible language of the heart.

Martin Luther King, Jr.

Judges

As for the safety of society, we commit honest mani-
acs to Bedlam, so judges should be withdrawn from
their bench, whose erroneous biases are leading us to
dissolution.

Thomas Jefferson

...it is better that we lose the services of the exceptions who are good Judges after they are seventy and
avoid the presence on the Bench of men who are not
able to keep up with the work, or to perform it satis-
factorily.

William Howard Taft

Judges, like people, may be divided roughly into four
classes: judges with neither head nor heart—they are
to be avoided at all costs; judges with head but no
heart—they are almost as bad; then judges with heart
but no head—risky but better than the first two; and
finally, those rare judges who possess both head and
a heart—thanks to blind luck, that's our judge.

Robert Traver

Judgment

But let judgment run down as waters, and righteousness as a mighty stream.

Amos 5:24.

Nature has but one judgment on wrong conduct—if
you can call that a judgment which seemingly has no
reference to conduct as such—the judgment of death.

Oliver Wendell Holmes

Judgment is forced upon us by experience.

Samuel Johnson

Judgment

Beware, so long as you live, of judging men by their outward appearance.

Jean de La Fontaine

If we could first know where we are, and whither we are tending, we could then better judge what to do, and how to do it.

Abraham Lincoln

We judge ourselves by what we feel capable of doing; others judge us by what we have done.

Henry Wadsworth Longfellow

Everyone complains of the badness of his memory, but nobody of his judgment.

Duc François de La Rochefoucauld

I mistrust the judgment of every man in a case in which his own wishes are concerned.

Arthur Wellesley, Duke of Wellington

One cool judgment is worth a thousand hasty counsels. The thing to be supplied is light, not heat.

Woodrow Wilson

Justice

Justice, voiceless, unseen, seeth thee when thou sleepest and when thou goest forth and when thou liest down. Continually doth she attend thee...

Aeschylus

Justice is itself the great standing policy of civil society; and any eminent departure from it, under any circumstances, lies under the suspicion of being no policy at all.

Edmund Burke

"No, no!" said the Queen. "Sentence first—verdict afterwards."

Lewis Carroll

Heaven gives long life to the just and the intelligent.

Confucius

Sir, I say that justice is truth in action.

Benjamin Disraeli

Though force can protect in emergency, only justice, fairness, consideration and cooperation can finally lead men to the dawn of eternal peace.

Dwight D. Eisenhower

That it is better 100 guilty Persons should escape than that one innocent Person should suffer, is a Maxim that has been long and generally approved.

Benjamin Franklin

Justice delayed is justice denied.

Attributed to William E. Gladstone

The achievement of justice is an endless process.

John F. Kennedy

He reminds me of the man who murdered both his parents, and then, when sentence was about to be pronounced, pleaded for mercy on the grounds that he was an orphan.

Abraham Lincoln

Man is unjust, but God is just; and finally justice triumphs.

Henry Wadsworth Longfellow

What doth the Lord require of thee, but to do justly, and to love mercy, and to walk humbly with thy God?

Micah 6:8.

Justice

Just as, in fact there can be no peace without order so there can be no order without justice.

Pope Pius XII

Salvation for a race, nation, or class must come from within. Freedom is never granted; it is won. Justice is never given; it is exacted.

A. Philip Randolph

Only the actions of the just
Smell sweet and blossom in the dust.

James Shirley

Thrice is he armed that hath his quarrel just, And he but naked, though licked up in steel, Whose conscience with injustice is corrupted.

Shakespeare

What's sauce for a goose is sauce for a gander.

Jonathan Swift

Judging from the main portions of the history of the world, so far, justice is always in jeopardy.

Walt Whitman

He that ruleth over men must be just.

Samuel 23:3

Justice in the life and conduct of the State is possible only as first it resides in the hearts and souls of the citizens.

Author unknown

Kindness

It is difficult to tell how much men's minds are conciliated by a kind manner and gentle speech.

Cicero

He who wishes to secure the good of others, has already secured his own.

Confucius

A kindness loses its grace by being noised abroad,
Who desires it to be remembered should forget it.

Pierre Corneille

A kind heart is a fountain of gladness, making everything in its vicinity freshen into smiles.

Washington Irving

To cultivate kindness is a valuable part of the business of life.

Samuel Johnson

I expect to pass through life but once. If therefore, there be any kindness I can show, or any good thing I can do to any fellow being, let me do it now, and not defer or neglect it, as I shall not pass this way again.

William Penn

It is a kindness to refuse gently what you intend to deny.

Publilius Syrus

This was the unkindest cut of all.

Shakespeare

Yet do I fear thy nature;
It is too full o' the milk of human kindness.

Shakespeare

Kings

His hands would plait the priest's guts, if he had no rope, to strangle kings.

Denis Diderot

Implements of war and subjugation are the last arguments to which kings resort.

Patrick Henry

Knowledge

What one knows is, in youth, of little moment; they know enough who know how to learn.

Henry Adams

Knowledge is, indeed, that which, next to virtue, truly and essentially raises one man above another.

Joseph Addison

A great deal of knowledge, which is not capable of making a man wise, has a natural tendency to make him vain and arrogant.

Joseph Addison

Knowledge is power.

Francis Bacon

The trouble with people is not that they dont know but that they know so much that ain't so.

Attributed to Josh Billings (Henry Wheeler Shaw)

What little I do know I hope I am certain of'.

Josh Billings

I honestly believe it is better to know nothing than to know what ain't so.

Josh Billings

Knowledge is a comfortable and necessary retreat and shelter for us in an advanced age; and if we do not plant it while young, it will give us no shade when we grow old.

Lord Chesterfield

Knowledge

No technical knowledge can outweigh knowledge of the humanities, in the gaining of which philosophy and history walk hand in hand.

Winston Churchill

The essence of knowledge is, having it, to apply it; not having it, to confess your ignorance.

Confucius

The more extensive a man's knowledge of what has been done, the greater will be his power of knowing what to do.

Benjamin Disraeli

If a man empties his purse into his head no one can take it away from him. An investment in knowledge always pays the best interest.

Attributed to Benjamin Franklin

It is the province of knowledge to speak, and it is the privilege of wisdom to listen.

Oliver Wendell Holmes

The benefits of education and of useful knowledge, generally diffused through a community, are essential to the preservation of a free government.

Attributed to Sam Houston

Knowledge is of two kinds. We know a subject ourselves or we know where we can find information upon it.

Samuel Johnson

Knowledge will forever govern ignorance: And a people who mean to be their own Governors, must arm themselves with the power which knowledge gives.

James Madison

Knowledge

To myself I seem to have been only like a boy playing on the seashore, and diverting myself in now and then finding a smoother pebble, or a prettier shell than ordinary, whilst the great ocean of truth lay all undiscovered before me.

Isaac Newton

Then I began to think, that it is very true which is commonly said, that the one–half of the world knoweth not how the other half liveth.

François Rabelais

...They never open their mouths without subtracting from the sum of human knowledge.

Thomas B. Reed

All I know is what I read in the papers.

Will Rogers

Knowledge comes, but wisdom lingers, ...

Alfred, Lord Tennyson

We have not the reverent feeling for the rainbow that a savage has, because we know how it is made. We have lost as much as we gained by prying into that matter.

Mark Twain

Labor

There is no right to strike against the public safety by anybody, anywhere, anytime.

Calvin Coolidge

Employment is nature's physician, and is essential to human happiness.

Galen

Don't waste any time mourning—organize!

Joe Hill

I've had the best possible chance of learning that what the working classes really need is to be allowed some part in the direction of public affairs, ...

Henrik Ibsen

Excellence in any department can be attained only by the labor of a lifetime; it is not to be purchased at a lesser price.

Samuel Johnson

Let them be hewers of wood and drawers of water.

Joshua 9:21

Each needs the other: capital cannot do without labor, nor labor without capital.

Pope Leo XIII

It ill behooves one who has supped at labor's table and who has been sheltered in labor's house to curse with equal fervor and fine impartiality both labor and its adversaries when they become locked in deadly embrace.

John L. Lewis

Labor is prior to, and independent of, capital. Capital is only the fruit of labor, and could never have existed if labor had not first existed.

Abraham Lincoln

The strongest bond of human sympathy, outside of the family relation, should be one uniting all working people, of all nations, and tongues, and kindreds.

Abraham Lincoln

The labourer is worthy of his hire.

Luke 10:7

Labor

Love, therefore, labor; if thou shouldst not want it for food, thou mayest for physic. It is wholesome to the body and good for the mind; it prevents the fruit of idleness.

William Penn

No business which depends for existence on paying less than living wages to its workers has any right to continue...

Franklin D. Roosevelt

I am a true labourer: I earn that I eat, get that I wear, owe no man hate, envy no man's happiness, glad of other men's good.

Shakespeare

There is no real wealth but the labor of man. Were the mountains of gold and the valleys of silver, the world would not be one grain of corn the richer; no one comfort would be added to the human race.

Percy B. Shelley

No race can prosper 'til it learns that there is as much dignity in tilling the field as in writing a poem.

Booker T. Washington

Employment gives health, sobriety and morals. Constant employment and well-paid labor produce, in a country like ours, general prosperity, content, and cheerfulness.

Daniel Webster

Language

Slovenly language corrodes the mind.

James Truslow Adams

Language is the armory of the human mind, and at once contains the trophies of its past and the weapons of its future conquests.

Samuel Taylor Coleridge

A man who does not know foreign languages is ignorant of his own.

Goethe

There is no master key to the inner life of a people, but language unlocks a vast treasure house.

Edgar Lee Hewett

Every language is a temple in which the soul of those who speak it is enshrined.

Oliver Wendell Holmes

Language is the dress of thought.

Samuel Johnson

England and America are two countries separated by the same language.

George Bernard Shaw

Language, as well as the faculty of speech, was the immediate gift of God.

Noah Webster

Laughter

You grow up the day you have the first real laugh—at yourself.

Ethel Barrymore

God hath not granted to woeful mortals even laughter without tears.

Callimachus

Laughter

No man who has once heartily and wholly laughed can be altogether and irreclaimably depraved.

Thomas Carlyle

Laughter is the tonic, the relief, the surcease for pain.

Charlie Chaplin

You no doubt laugh in your sleeve.

Cicero

As the crackling of thorns under a pot, so is the laughter of a fool.

Ecclesiastes 7:6

The loud laugh that spoke the vacant mind.

Oliver Goldsmith

Laughter unquenchable arose among the blessed gods.

Homer

Laughing is the sensation of feeling good all over, and showing it principally in one spot.

Bob Hope

I laugh because I must not cry.

Abraham Lincoln

Woe unto you that laugh now! for ye shall niourn and weep.

Luke 6:25

There are three things which are real: God, human folly, and laughter. Since the first two pass our comprehension, we must do what we can with the third.

Aubrey Menen

He deserves Paradise who makes his companions laugh.

Mohammed

Everything gives cause for either laughter or tears.

Seneca

The pleasantest laughter is at the expense of our enemies.

Sophocles

Laughter is not a bad beginning for a friendship, and it is the best ending for one.

Oscar Wilde

Law

A government of laws and not of men.

John Adams

Law is a Bottomless Pit, it is a Cormorant, a Harpy, that devours every thing.

John Arbuthnot

Law is a pledge that the citizens of a state will do justice to one another.

Aristotle

Any law that takes hold of a man's daily life cannot prevail in a community unless the vast majority of the community are actively in favor of it. The laws that are the most operative are the laws which protect life.

Henry Ward Beecher

A law is valuable not because it is law, but because there is right in it.

Henry Ward Beecher

The laws place the safety of all before the safety of individuals.

Cicero

Law

Men would be great criminals did they need as many laws as they make.

Charles John Darling

He that keepeth the law of the Lord getteth the understanding thereof: and the perfection of the fear of the Lord is wisdom.

Ecclesiasticus 21:11.

If you like laws and sausages, you should never watch either one being made.

Attributed to Otto Von Bismarck

So great moreover is the regard of the law for private property, that it will not authorize the least violation of it; no, not even for the general good of the whole community.

William Blackstone

Law is the embodiment of the moral sentiment of the people.

William Blackstone

The law is a causeway upon which so long as he keeps to it a citizen may walk safely.

Robert Bolt

Men do not make laws. They do but discover them.

Calvin Coolidge

Time is the best interpreter of every doubtful law.

Dionysius of Halicarnassus

If one man can be allowed to determine for himself what is law, every man can. That means first chaos, then tyranny. Legal process is an essential part of the democratic process.

Justice Felix Frankfurter

Possession is nine points of the law.

Thomas Fuller

It cannot be helped, it is as it should be, that the law is behind the times.

Oliver Wendell Holmes

Compassion to an offender who has grossly violated the laws, is, in effect, a cruelty to the peaceable subject who has observed them.

Junius

Act only according to that maxim by which you can at the same time will that it should become a universal law.

Immanuel Kant

In law a man is guilty when he violates the rights of another. In ethics he is guilty if he only thinks of doing so.

Immanuel Kant

Ye shall have one manner of law, as well for the stranger, as for one of your own country.

Leviticus 24:22

Because just as good morals, if they are to be maintained, have need of the laws, so the laws, if they are to be observed, have need of good morals.

Niccolò Machiavelli

The purpose of law is to prevent the strong from always having their way.

Ovid

No man is above the law and no man is below it; nor do we ask any man's permission when we require him to obey it.

Theodore Roosevelt

Law

Where is there any book of the law so clear to each man as that written in his heart?

Leo Tolstoy

Lawyers

America is the paradise of lawyers.

Attributed to David J. Brewer

He that pleads his own cause has a fool for his client.

English Proverb

The idea of having a lawyer present before you can ask a man a question about whether he has committed a crime is taking absurdity to the extreme.

John L. McClellan

The first thing we do, let's kill all the lawyers.

Shakespeare

Leadership

I light my candle from their torches.

Robert Burton

And when we think we lead we most are led.

Lord Byron

There go the people. I must follow them, for I am their leader.

Attributed to Alexandre Ledru–Rollin

The final test of a leader is that he leaves behind him in other men the conviction and the will to carry on.

Walter Lippmann

You cannot be a leader and ask other people to follow you, unless you know how to follow, too.

Sam Rayburn

An two men ride of a horse, one must ride behind.
Shakespeare

Ill can he rule the great that cannot reach the small.
Edmund Spenser

Reason and calm judgment, the qualities specially belonging to a leader.

Tacitus

Some citizens are so good that nothing a leader can do will make them better. Others are so incorrigible that nothing can be done to improve them. But the great bulk of the people go with the moral tide of the moment. The leader must help create that tide.

Author unknown

Learning

What one knows is, in youth, of little moment; they know enough who know how to learn.

Henry Adams

All men by nature desire to know.

Aristotle

Learning teaches how to carry things in suspense, without prejudice, till you resolve.

Francis Bacon

That there should one man die ignorant who had capacity for knowledge, this I call tragedy.

Thomas Carlyle

Wear your learning, like your watch, in a private pocket; and do not pull it out, and strike it, merely to show that you have one.

Lord Chesterfield

Learning

Acquire new knowledge whilst thinking over the old, and you may become a teacher of others.

Confucius

A smattering of everything and a knowledge of nothing.

Charles Dickens

Seeing much, suffering much, and studying much, are the three pillars of learning.

Benjamin Disraeli

Education is a controlling grace to the young, consolation to the old, wealth to the poor, and ornament to the rich.

Diogenes Laertius

You send your child to the schoolmaster, but 'tis the schoolboys who educate him.

Ralph Waldo Emerson

If you have knowledge, let others light their candles at it.

Margaret Fuller

A child's education should begin at least one hundred years before he was born.

Oliver Wendell Holmes

The important thing is not so much that every child should be taught, as that every child should be given the wish to learn.

John Lubbock

A little learning is a dangerous thing;
Drink deep, or taste not the Pierian spring:
There shallow draughts intoxicate the brain,
And drinking largely sobers us again.

Alexander Pope

'Tis education forms the common mind: Just as the twig is bent the tree's inclined.

Alexander Pope

The great aim of education is not knowledge but action.

Herbert Spencer

It is well to learn caution by the misfortunes of others.

Publilius Syrus

There is no royal road to learning; no short cut to the acquirement of any valuable art.

Anthony Trollope

Legislators

In all forms of government the people is the true legislator.

Edmund Burke

Legislators represent people, not trees or acres. Legislators are elected by voters, not farms or cities or economic interests.

Earl Warren

Parliament will train you to talk; and above all things to hear, with patience, unlimited quantities of foolish talk.

Thomas Carlyle

The commons, faithful to their system, remained in a wise and masterly inactivity.

James Mackintosh

No man's life, liberty or property are safe while the Legislature is in session.

Quoted by Gideon J. Tucker

Leisure

The aim of education is the wise use of leisure.

Aristotle

When a man's busy, why, leisure Strikes him as wonderful pleasure; 'Faith, and at leisure once is he? Straightway he wants to be busy.

Robert Browning

He does not seem to me to be a free man who does not sometimes do nothing.

Cicero

It is the mark of a superior man that he will take no harmful ease.

Confucius

A life of leisure and a life of laziness are two things.

Ben Franklin

Give time to your friends, leisure to your wife, relax your mind, give rest to your body, so that you may the better fulfil your accustomed occupation.

Phaedrus

To be able to fill leisure intelligently is the last product of civilization.

Bertrand Russell

Liberty

This liberty will look easy by and by when nobody dies to get it.

Maxwell Anderson

The United States appear to be destined by Providence to plague America with misery in the name of liberty.

Attributed to Simón Bolívar

Men are qualified for civil liberty in exact proportion to their disposition to put moral chains upon their own appetites...

Edmund Burke

The people never give up their liberties but under some delusion.

Edmund Burke

The true danger is when liberty is nibbled away, for expedients, and by parts.

Edmund Burke

True liberty consists only in the power of doing what we ought to will, and in not being constrained to do what we ought not to will.

Attributed to Jonathan Edwards

Those who would give up essential Liberty, to purchase a little temporary Safety, deserve neither Liberty nor Safety.

Benjamin Franklin

Civil liberty is only natural liberty, modified and secured by the sanctions of civil society. It is not a thing, in its own nature, precarious and dependent on human will and caprice; but it is conformable to the constitution of man, as well as necessary to the well-being of society.

Alexander Hamilton

Liberty lies in the hearts of men and women; when it dies there, no constitution, no law, no court can save it; no constitution, no law, no court can even do much to help it...

Learned Hand

Liberty

What would they have? Is life so dear, or peace so sweet, as to be purchased at the price of chains and slavery? Forbid it, Almighty God! —I know not what course others may take; but as for me, give me liberty, or give me death!

Patrick Henry

The spark of liberty in the mind and spirit of man cannot be long extinguished; it will break into flames that will destroy every coercion which seems to limit it.

Herbert Hoover

The God who gave us life gave us liberty at the same time.

Thomas Jefferson

It behoves every man who values liberty of conscience for himself, to resist invasions of it in the case of others; or their case may, by change of circumstances, become his own.

Thomas Jefferson

The tree of liberty must be refreshed from time to time with the blood of patriots and tyrants. It is it's natural manure.

Thomas Jefferson

The inescapable price of liberty is an ability to preserve it from destruction.

General Douglas Macarthur

The struggle between Liberty and Authority is the most conspicuous feature in the portions of history with which we are earliest familiar, particularly in that of Greece, Rome, and England.

John Stuart Mill

He that would make his own liberty secure, must guard even his enemy from oppression; for if he violates this duty, he establishes a precedent that will reach to himself.

Thomas Paine

Eternal vigilance is the price of liberty—power is ever stealing from the many to the few... The hand entrusted with power becomes ... the necessary enemy of the people.

Wendell Phillips,

Liberty means responsibility. That is why most men dread it.

George Bernard Shaw

The men of the future will yet fight their way to many a liberty that we do not even miss.

Max Sterner

There is ... no liberty but liberty under law. Law does not restrict liberty; it creates the only real liberty there is.

William Sumner

For the saddest epitaph which can be carved in memory of a vanished liberty is that it was lost because its possessors failed to stretch forth a saving hand while yet there was time.

George Sutherland

The contest, for ages, has been to rescue Liberty from the grasp of executive power.

Daniel Webster

God grants liberty only to those who love it, and are always ready to guard and defend it.

Daniel Webster

Liberty

The history of liberty is a history of resistance. The history of liberty is a history of the limitation of governmental power, not the increase of it.

Woodrow Wilson

Life

Age and youth look upon life from the opposite ends of the telescope; to the one it is exceedingly long, to the other exceedingly short.

Henry Ward Beecher

All of the animals, excepting man, know that the principal business of life is to enjoy it.

Samuel Butler

Life is a test and this world a place of trial. Always the problems—or it may be the same problem—will be presented to every generation in different forms.

Winston Churchill

I have measured out my life with coffee spoons.

T. S. Eliot

What is life but the angle of vision? A man is measured by the angle at which he looks at objects.

Ralph Waldo Emerson

The fool, with all his other faults, has this also: he is always getting ready to live.

Epicurus

Were it offered to my choice, I should have no objection to a repetition of the same life from its beginnings, only asking the advantages authors have in a second edition to correct some faults.

Benjamin Franklin

...The fullness of life is in the hazards of life. And, at the worst, there is that in us which can turn defeat into victory.

Edith Hamelton

I think that, as life is action and passion, it is required of a man that he should share the passion and action of his time at peril of being judged not to have lived.

Oliver Wendell Holmes

Life is a romantic business. It is painting a picture, not doing a sum—but you have to make the romance, and it will come to the question how much fire you have in your belly.

Oliver Wendell Holmes

The mind that is cheerful at present will have no solicitude for the future, and will meet the bitter occurrences of life with a smile.

Horace

...the giver of life, who gave it for happiness and not for wretchedness.

Thomas Jefferson

Yes! Life is a banquet, and most poor sons-of-bitches are starving to death! Live!

Jerome Lawrence and Robert E. Lee

Unrest of spirit is a mark of life; one problem after another presents itself and in the solving of them we can find our greatest pleasure.

Karl Menninger

As for man, his days are as grass: as a flower of the field, so he flourisheth.

Psalms 8:15

Life

Life is not so important as the duties of life.
John Randolph

I wish to preach, not the doctrine of ignoble ease, but the doctrine of the strenuous life.
Theodore Roosevelt

A baby is God's opinion that life should go on.
Carl Sandburg

Life is neither a good nor an evil; it is simply the place where good and evil exist.
Seneca

Life is as tedious as a twice–told tale, Vexing the dull ear of a drowsy man.
Shakespeare

One man in his time plays many parts, His acts being seven ages.
Shakespeare

The web of our life is of a mingled yam, good and ill together.
Shakespeare

Anyone can carry his burden, however hard, until nightfall. Anyone can do his work, however hard, for one day. Anyone can live sweetly, patiently, lovingly, purely, till the sun goes down. And this is all that life really means.
Attributed to Robert Louis Stevenson

If a man is alive, there is always *danger* that he may die, though the danger must be allowed to be less in proportion as he is dead and alive to begin with. A man sits as many risks as he runs.
Henry David Thoreau

The mass of men lead lives of quiet desperation.

Henry David Thoreau

Let us so live that when we come to die even the undertaker will be sorry.

Mark Twain

Living

There are obviously two educations. One should teach us how to make a living and the other how to live.

James Truslow Adams

It is not well for a man to pray cream and live skim milk.

Henry Ward Beecher

Man doth not live by bread only, but by every word that proceedeth out of the mouth of the Lord doth man live.

Deuteronomy 8;3

Never complain and never explain

Benjamin Disraeli

I would rather be ashes than dust! I would rather that my spark should burn out in a brilliant blaze than it should be stifled by dry-rot. I would rather be a superb meteor, every atom of me in magnificent glow, than a sleepy and permanent planet. The proper function of man is to live, not to exist. I shall not waste my days in trying to prolong them. I shall use my time.

Jack London

Man is born to live, not to prepare for life.

Boris Pasternak

Living

Only those are fit to live who do not fear to die; and none are fit to die who have shrunk from the joy of life and the duty of life. Both life and death are parts of the same Great Adventure.

Theodore Roosevelt

Let us endeavor so to live that when we come to die even the undertaker will be sorry.

Mark Twain

Loneliness

It is loneliness that makes the loudest noise. This is as true of men as of dogs.

Eric Hoffer

All this hideous doubt, despair, and dark confusion of the soul a lonely man must know, for he is united to no image save that which he creates himself.

Thomas Wolfe

Love

True love is eternal, infinite, and always like itself. It is equal and pure, without violent demonstrations: it is seen with white hairs and is always young in the heart.

Honoré de Balzac

How do I love thee? Let me count the ways.
I love thee with a love I seemed to lose
With my lost saints, —I love thee with the breath,
Smiles, tears, of all my life! —If God choose,
I shall but love thee better after death.

Elizabeth B. Browning

Love

God be thanked, the meanest of his creatures
Boasts two soul-sides, one to face the world with,
One to show a woman when he loves her.

Robert Browning

Oh my luve's like a red, red, rose,
That's newly sprung in June;
Oh my luve's like the melodie
That's sweetly played in tune.

Robert Burns

To see her is to love her,
And love but her forever;
For nature made her what she is,
And never made anither!

Robert Burns

Alas! the love of women! it is known To be a lovely and
a fearful thing.

Lord Byron

Love and war are the same thing, and stratagems and
policy are as allowable in the one as in the other.

Cervantes

If love be good, from whennes comth my wo?

Geoffrey Chaucer

The Stoics define love as the endeavor to form a
friendship inspired by beauty.

Cicero

When povertie comes in at doores, love leaps out at
windowes.

John Clark

Say what you will, 'tis better to be left Than never to
have loved.

William Congreve

Love

We are all born for love... It is the principle of existence and its only end.

Benjamin Disraeli

Men and women call one another inconstant, and accuse one another of having changed their minds, when, God knows, they have but changed the object of their eye, and seen a better white or red.

John Donne

But you must believe me when I tell you that I have found it impossible to carry the heavy burden of responsibility and to discharge my duties as King as I would wish to do without the help and support of the woman I love.

Edward VIII

All mankind love a lover.

Ralph Waldo Emerson

He is not a lover who does not love forever.

Euripides

Perhaps they were right in putting love into books...
Perhaps it could not live anywhere else.

William Faulkner

For, you see, each day I love you more,
Today more than yesterday and less than tomorrow.

Rosemonde Gérard

Love has power that dispels Death; charm that conquers the enemy.

Kahlil Gibran

Love grants in a moment
What toil can hardly achieve in an age.

Goethe

Ah! What is love?
It is a pretty thing,
As sweet unto a shepherd as a king,
And sweeter too;
For kings have cares that wait upon a crown,
And cares can make the sweetest love to frown.

Robert Greene

To demand of love that it be without jealousy is to ask of light that it cast no shadows.

Oscar Hammling

All brave men love; for he only is brave who has affections to fight for, whether in the daily battle of life, or in physical contests.

Nathaniel Hawthorne

Whom the Lord loveth he chasteneth.

Hebrews 12:6

If you would be loved, love.

Hecato

Who love too much, hate in the like extreme.

Homer

A women is more considerate in affairs of love than a man; because love is more the study and business of her life.

Washington Irving

Greater love hath no man than this, that a man lay down his life for his friends.

John 15:13

There is no fear in love; but perfect love casteth out fear.

I John 4:8

Love

Love in a hut, with water and a crust,
Is—love, forgive us!—cinders, ashes, dust.
John Keats

Come live with me and be my love,
And we will all the pleasures prove,
That valleys, groves, or hills, or fields,
Or woods and steepy mountains yields.
Christopher Marlowe

'Tis not love's going hurts my days,
But that it went in little ways.
Edna St. Vincent Millay

Take love away from life and you take away its pleasures.
Molière

'Tis sweet to think, that, where'er we rove,
We are sure to find something blissful and dear;
And when we're far from the lips we love,
We've but to make love to the lips we are near.
Thomas Moore

Love is indeed heaven upon earth; since heaven above would not be heaven without it; ...
William Penn

If all the world and love were young,
And truth in every shepherd's tongue,
These pretty pleasures might me move
To live with thee, and be thy love.
Sir Walter Raleigh

The pleasure of love is in loving; and we are much happier in the passion we feel than in that which we inspire.
François de la Rochefoucauld

Whither thou goest, I will go; and where thou lodgest, I will lodge: thy people shall be my people, and thy God my God.

Ruth 1:16

No sooner met but they looked, no sooner looked but they loved, no sooner loved but they sighed, no sooner sighed but they asked one another the reason.

Shakespeare

Where love is great, the littlest doubts are fear;
When little fears grow great, great love grows there.

Shakespeare

But love is blind, and lovers cannot see
The pretty follies that themselves commit.

Shakespeare

Ay me! for aught that I ever could read,
Could ever hear by tale or history,
The course of true love never did run smooth.

Shakespeare

Speak low, if you speak love.

Shakespeare

There is no creature loves me,
And if I die, no soul shall pity me.

Shakespeare

First love is only a little foolishness and a lot of curiosity: no really self-respecting woman would take advantage of it.

George Bernard Shaw

Love is a symbol of eternity. It wipes out all sense of time, destroying all memory of a beginning and all fear of an end.

Madame de Statl

Love

And blessings on the falling out
That all the more endears,
When we fall out with those we love,
And kiss again with tears.

Alfred, Lord Tennyson

I hold it true, whate'er befall;
I feel it, when I sorrow most;
'Tis better to have loved and lost
Than never to have loved at all.

Alfred, Lord Tennyson

To say that you can love one person all your life is just like saying that one candle will continue burning as long as you live.

Leo Tolstoy

Beware of her fair locks, for when she winds them round a young man's neck, she will not set him free again.

Johann Wolfgang von Goethe

Loyalty

If put to the pinch, an ounce of loyalty is worth a pound of cleverness.

Elbert Hubbard

Up to a certain point it is good for us to know that there are people in the world who will give us love and unquestioned loyalty to the limit of their ability. I doubt, however, if it is good for us to feel assured of this without the accompanying obligation of having to justify this devotion by our behavior.

Eleanor Roosevelt

Loyalty means nothing unless it has at its heart the absolute principle of self-sacrifice.

Woodrow Wilson

Luxury

Luxury and avarice—these pests have been the ruin of every state.

Cato

Faint-hearted men are the fruit of luxurious countries. The same soil never produces both luxuries and heroes.

Herodotus

We act as though comfort and luxury were the chief requirements of life, when all that we need to make us really happy is something to be enthusiastic about.

Charles Kingsley

Fell luxury! more perilous to youth
Than storms or quicksands, poverty, or chains

Hannah More

People have declaimed against luxury for 2000 years, in verse and in prose, and people have always delighted in it.

Voltaire

On the soft beds of luxury most kingdoms have expired.

Edward Young

Majority

A majority can do anything.

Joseph G. Cannon

Majority

One with the law is a majority.

Calvin Coolidge

One and God make a majority.

Frederick Douglass

The oppression of a majority is detestable and odious: the oppression of a minority is only by one degree less detestable and odious.

William Ewart Gladstone

It is my principle that the will of the majority should always prevail.

Thomas Jefferson

How a minority,
Reaching majority,
Siezing authority,
Hates a minority!

Attributed to Leonard Harman Robbins

The thing we have to fear in this country,
to my way of thinking, is the influence of the
organized minorities, ...

Alfred E. Smith

Malice

Malice is cunning.

Cicero

Malice hath a strong memory.

Thomas Fuller

With malice toward none; with charity for all; with firmness in the right, as God gives us to see the right, let us strive on to finish the work we are in.

Abraham Lincoln

Man

Man perfected by society is the best of all animals; he is the most terrible of all when he lives without law, and without justice.

Aristotle

This Being of mine, whatever it really is, consists of a little flesh, a little breath and the ruling Reason.

Marcus Aurelius

Men commonly think according to their inclinations, speak according to their learning and imbibed opinions, but generally act according to custom.

Francis Bacon

There are times when one would like to hang the whole human race, and finish the farce.

Mark Twain

Man is a fallen god who remembers the heavens.

Alphonse de Lamartine

The poet's voice need not merely be the record of man, it can be one of the props, the pillars to help him endure and prevail.

William Faulkner

Who is wise? *He that learns from every One.* Who is powerful? *He that governs his Passions.* Who is rich? *He that is content.* Who is that? *Nobody.*

Benjamin Franklin

We all are blind until we see
That in the human plan
Nothing is worth the making if
It does not make the man.

Edwin Markham

Man

Men are men before they are lawyers, or physicians, or merchants, or manufacturers; and if you make them capable and sensible men, they will make themselves capable and sensible lawyers or physicians.

John Stuart Mill

Man is a rope stretched between the animal and the superman—a rope over an abyss.

Friedrich W. Nietzsche

Man, created to God's image and likeness is not just flesh and blood. The sexual instinct is not all that he has. Man is also, and preeminently, intelligent and free; and thanks to these powers he is, and must remain, superior to the rest of creation; they give him mastery over his physical, psychological and affective appetites.

Pope Paul VI

A great man left a watchword that we can well repeat: "There is no indispensable man."

Franklin D. Roosevelt

When I die, my epitaph or whatever you call those signs on gravestones is going to read: "I joked about every prominent man of my time, but I never met a man I didn't like." I am so proud of that I can hardly wait to die so it can be carved. And when you come to my grave you will find me sitting there, proudly reading it.

Will Rogers

The awareness that we are all human beings together has become lost in war and through politics.

Albert Schweitzer

Who shall enumerate the many ways in which that costly piece of fixed capital, a human being, may be employed! More of him is wanted everywhere! Hunt, then, for some situation in which your humanity may be used.

Albert Schweitzer

All the world's a stage,
And all the men and women merely players.
They have their exits and their entrances,
And one man in his time plays many parts, . . .

Shakespeare

   ...man, proud man,
Dress'd in a little brief authority, ...

Shakespeare

He was a man, take him for all in all, I shall not look upon his like again.

Shakespeare

How beauteous mankind is! O brave new world, That has such people in 't!

Shakespeare

Every man will be a poet if he can; otherwise a philosopher or man of science. This proves the superiority of the poet.

Henry David Thoreau

Man's capacities have never been measured; nor are we to judge of what he can do by any precedents, so little has been tried.

Henry David Thoreau

Mankind which began in a cave and behind a windbreak will end in the disease–soaked ruins of a slum.

H. G. Wells

Marriage

He that hath a wife and children hath given hostages to fortune; for they are impediments to great enterprises, either of virtue or mischief.

Francis Bacon

He was reputed one of the wise men that made answer to the question when a man should marry? "A young man not yet, an elder man not at all."

Francis Bacon

Marriage and hanging go by destiny; matches are made in heaven.

Robert Burton

The first bond of society is marriage; the next, our children; then the whole family and all things in common.

Cicero

Thus grief still treads upon the heels of pleasure,
Marry'd in haste, we may repent at leisure.

William Congreve

I have always thought that every woman should marry, and no man.

Benjamin Disraeli

A single man has not nearly the value he would have in a state of union. He is an incomplete animal. He resembles the odd half of a pair of scissors.

Benjamin Franklin

Happy and thrice happy are they who enjoy an uninterrupted union, and whose love, unbroken by any complaints, shall not dissolve until the last day.

Horace

A gentleman who had been very unhappy in marriage, married immediately after his wife died: Johnson said, it was the triumph of hope over experience.

Samuel Johnson

Hail, wedded love, mysterious law; true source Of human offspring.

John Milton

If you would marry wisely, marry your equal.

Ovid

Men dream in courtship, but in wedlock wake.

Alexander Pope

Marriage is one long conversation chequered by disputes.

Robert Louis Stevenson

All happy families resemble one another; every unhappy family is unhappy in its own fashion.

Leo Tolstoy

Men marry because they are tired; women because they are curious. Both are disappointed.

Oscar Wilde

Memory

Joy's recollection is no longer joy, while sorrow's memory is sorrow still.

Lord Byron

To be ignorant of what happened before you were born is to be ever a child. For what is man's lifetime unless the memory of past events is woven with those of earlier times.

Cicero

Memory

Memory is the receptacle and sheath of all knowledge.
Cicero

There is no greater sorrow than to recall, in misery, the time when we were happy.

Dante

Creditors have better memories than debtors; they are a superstitious sect, great observers of set days and times.

Benjamin Franklin

Memory is the treasure–house of the mind.
Thomas Fuller

We can remember minutely and precisely only the things which never really happened to us.
Eric Hoffer

A retentive memory is a good thing, but the ability to forget is the true token of greatness.
Elbert Hubbard

The true art of memory is the art of attention.
Samuel Johnson

Women and elephants never forget.
Dorothy Parker

Better by far you should forget and smile,
Than that you should remember and be sad.
Christina Rossetti

Remember thee!
Ay, thou poor ghost, while memory holds a seat
In this distracted globe. Remember thee!
Yea, from the fable of my memory
I'll wipe away all trivial fond records.

Shakespeare

When to the sessions of sweet silent thought
I summon up remembrance of things past,
I sigh the lack of many a thing I sought,
And old woes new wail my dear time's waste.

Shakespeare

The Right Honourable Gentleman is indebted to his
memory for his jests, and to his imagination for his
facts.

Richard Brinsley Sheridan

Mercy

Mercy to him that shows it, is the rule.

William Cowper

Mercy more becomes a magistrate than the vindictive
wrath which men call justice.

Henry Wadsworth Longfellow

Blessed are the merciful: for they shall obtain mercy.

Matthew 5:7

What doth the Lord require of thee, but to do justly,
and to love mercy, and to walk humbly with thy God.

Micah 4:4

To hide the fault I see:
That mercy I to others show
That mercy show to me.

Alexander Pope

The quality of mercy is not strain'd
It droppeth as the gentle rain from heaven
Upon the place beneath: it is twice blest;
It blesseth him that gives and him that takes; ...

Shakespeare

229

Military

...number itself in armies importeth not much, where
the people is of weak courage; for, as Virgil saith, "It
never troubles the wolf how many the sheep be."

Francis Bacon

We must train and classify the whole of our male citizens, and make military instruction a regular part of
collegiate education.

Thomas Jefferson

No man who is not willing to bear arms and to fight
for his rights can give a good reason why he should be
entitled to the privilege of living in a free community.

Theodore Roosevelt

Nothing can be more hurtful to the service, than the
neglect of discipline; for that discipline, more than
numbers, gives one army the superiority over another.

George Washington

To know when to retreat; and to *dare* to do it.

Arthur Wellesley, Duke of Wellington

With willing hearts and skillful hands, the difficult we
do at once; the impossible takes a bit longer.

Author Unknown

Mind

Old minds are like old horses; you must exercise them
if you wish to keep them in working order.

John Quincy Adams

Generally speaking, poverty of speech is the outward
evidence of poverty of mind.

Bruce Barton

As the mind must govern the hands, so in every society the man of intelligence must direct the man of labor.

Samuel Johnson

A foolish consistency is the hobgoblin of little minds, adored by little statesmen and philosophers and divines.

Ralph Waldo Emerson

The mind is never satisfied with the objects immediately before it, but is always breaking away from the present moment, and losing itself in schemes of future felicity. ... The natural flights of the human mind are not from pleasure to pleasure, but from hope to hope.

Samuel Johnson

If there is anything in the world that can really be called a man's property, it is surely that which is the result of his mental activity.

Attributed to Arthur Schopenhauer

As the soil, however rich it may be, cannot be productive without culture, so the mind without cultivation can never produce good fruit.

Seneca

I not only use all the brains I have, but all I can borrow.

Woodrow Wilson

Moderation

The pursuit, even of the best things, ought to be calm and tranquil.

Cicero

Moderation

Everything that exceeds the bounds of moderation, has an unstable foundation.

Seneca

Money

Money is power, and you ought to be reasonably ambitious to have it.

Russell H. Conwell

The use of money is all the advantage there is in having it.

Benjamin Franklin

Money is a handmaiden, if thou knowest how to use it; a mistress, if thou knowest not.

Horace

In truth, the gold standard is already a barbarous relic.

John Maynard Keynes

Money is not required to buy one necessity of the soul.

Henry David Thoreau

He who tampers with the currency robs labor of its bread.

Daniel Webster

Morality

Every young man would do well to remember that all successful business stands on the foundation of morality.

Henry Ward Beecher

Too many moralists begin with a dislike of reality: a dislike of men as they are.

Clarence Shepard Day, Jr.

For what end shall we be connected with men, of whom this is the character and conduct? ... Is it, that we may see our wives and daughters the victims of legal prostitution; soberly dishonoured; speciously polluted; the outcasts of delicacy and virtue, and the lothing of God and man?

Timothy Dwight

There can by no high civility without a deep morality.

Ralph Waldo Emerson

Dante once said that the hottest places in hell are reserved for those who in a period of moral crisis maintain their neutrality.

John F. Kennedy

Mortality

I wrote my name upon the sand,
And trusted it would stand for aye;
But, soon, alas! the refluent sea
Had washed my feeble lines away

Horatio Alger, Jr.

The paths of glory lead but to the grave.

Thomas Gray

Don't strew me with roses after I'm dead.
When Death claims the light of my brow,
No flowers of life will cheer me: instead
You may give me my roses now!

Thomas F. Healey

Mortality

So fleet the works of men, back to their earth again;
Ancient and holy things fade like a dream.

Charles Kingsley

It is said an Eastern monarch once charged his wise
men to invent him a sentence, to be ever in view, and
which should be true and appropriate in all times and
situations. They presented him the words: "And *this,
too, shall pass away.*"

Abraham Lincoln

Music

Music, the greatest good that mortals know,
And all of heaven we have below.

Joseph Addison

Music exalts each joy, allays each grief,
Expels diseases, softens every pain,
Subdues the rage of poison, and the plague.

John Armstrong

Music is the mediator between the spiritual and the
sensual life.

Ludwig van Beethoven

Music is well said to be the speech of angels.

Thomas Carlyle

Music hath charms to soothe the savage breast,
To soften rocks, or bend a knotted oak.

William Congreve

It is not necessary to understand music; it is only
necessary that one enjoy it.

Leopold Stokowski

Nation

Happy are all free peoples,
  too strong to be dispossessed.
But blessed are those among nations
  who dare to be strong for the rest!
Elizabeth Barrett Browning

Great nations rise and fall. The people go from bondage to spiritual truth, to great courage, from courage to liberty, from liberty to abundance, from abundance to selfishness, from selfishness to complacency, from complacency to apathy, from apathy to dependence, from dependence back again to bondage.
Attributed to Benjamin Disraeli

How much more are men than nations!
Ralph Waldo Emerson

It is because nations tend to stupidity and baseness that mankind moves so slowly; it is because individuals have a capacity for better things that it moves at all.

George Gissing

The first panacea for a mismanaged nation is inflation of the currency; the second is war. Both bring a temporary prosperity; both bring a permanent ruin. But both are the refuge of political and economic opportunists.

Ernest Hemingway

There is no such thing as a little country. The greatness of a people is no more determined by their number than the greatness of a man is determined by his height.

Victor Hugo

Nation

A little one shall be come a thousand and a small one a strong nation.

Isaiah 9:22

The behavior of nations over a long period of time is the most reliable, though not the only, index of their national interest.

Walter Lippmann

Great nations write their autobiographies in three manuscripts, the book of their deeds, the book of their words and the book of their art. Not one of these books can be understood unless we read the two others, but of the three the only trustworthy one is the last.

John Ruskin

The political life of a nation is only the most superficial aspect of its being. In order to know its inner life, the source of its action, one must penetrate to its soul by literature, philosophy and the arts, where are reflected the ideas, the passions, the dreams of a whole people.

Romain Rolland

That nation is worthless which does not joyfully stake everything in defense of her honor.

Schiller

It is a maxim founded on the universal experience of mankind that no nation is to be trusted farther than it is bound by its interest.

George Washington

No nation is fit to sit in judgment upon any other nation.

Woodrow Wilson

Nature

There is not, in my opinion, anything more mysterious in nature than this instinct in animals, which thus rise above reason, and yet fall infinitely short of it.

Joseph Addison

The study of Nature is intercourse with the Highest Mind. You should never trifle with Nature.

Jean Louis Agassiz

All that thy seasons, O Nature, bring is fruit for me! All things come from thee, subsist in thee, go back to thee.

Marcus Aurelius

Believe one who knows: you will find something greater in woods than in books. Trees and stones will teach you that which you can never learn from masters.

St. Bernard of Clairvaux

Whatever befalls in accordance with Nature shall be accounted good.

Cicero

Nor rural sounds alone, but rural sounds,
Exhilarate the spirit, and restore
The tone of languid Nature.

William Cowper

Hast thou named all the birds without a gun;
Loved the wood-rose, and left it on its stalk?

Ralph Waldo Emerson

Nature is too thin a screen; the glory of the omnipresent God bursts through everywhere.

Ralph Waldo Emerson

Nature

Never does Nature say one thing and Wisdom another.

Juvenal

So Nature deals with us, and takes away
Our playthings one by one, and by the hand
Leads us to rest.

Henry Wadsworth Longfellow

In those vernal seasons of the year, when the air is
calm and pleasant, it were an injury and sullenness
against Nature not to go out and see her riches and
partake in her rejoicing with heaven and earth.

John Milton

The perfections of Nature show that she is the image
of God; her defects show that she is only his image.

Blaise Pascal

All Nature is but Art, unknown to thee;
All Chance, Direction, which thou canst not see.

Alexander Pope

Nature abhors a vacuum.

François Rabelais

And this our life, exempt from public haunt,
Finds tongues in trees, books in the running brooks,
Sermons in stones, and good in everything.

Shakespeare

One touch of nature makes the whole world kin.

Shakespeare

I inhale great draughts of space,
The east and the west are mine,
        and the north and the south are mine.
I am larger than I thought,
I did not know I held so much goodness.

Walt Whitman

Newspapers

Four hostile newspapers are more to be feared than a thousand bayonets.

Napoleon Bonaparte

For the newspaper is in all literalness the bible of democracy, the book out of which a people determines its conduct. It is the only serious book most people read. It is the only book they read every day.

Walter Lippmann

I generalized rashly: That is what kills political writing, this absurd pretence that you are delivering a great utterance. ... You are just a puzzled man making notes about what you think. ... You are drawing sketches in the sand which the sea will wash away.

Walter Lippmann

So I became a newspaperman. I hated to do it but I couldn't find honest employment.

Attributed to Mark Twain

Opinion

Every man has a right to his opinion, but no man has a right to be wrong in his facts.

Attributed to Bernard M. Baruch

There is probably an element of malice in the readiness to overestimate people; we are laying up for ourselves the pleasure of later cutting them down to size.

Eric Hoffer

A great many people think they are thinking when they are merely rearranging their prejudices.

Attributed to William James

Opinion

For the great enemy of the truth is very often not the lie—deliberate, contrived, and dishonest—but the myth—persistent, persuasive, and unrealistic.

John F. Kennedy

We cannot ask a man what he will do, and if we should, and he should answer us, we should despise him for it. Therefore we must take a man whose opinions are known.

Abraham Lincoln

This imputation of inconsistency is one to which every sound politician and every honest thinker must sooner or later subject himself. The foolish and the dead alone never change their opinion.

James Russell Lowell

There are as many opinions as there are experts.

Franklin D. Roosevelt

The opinions that are held with passion are always those for which no good ground exists; indeed the passion is the measure of the holder's lack of rational conviction. Opinions in politics and religion are almost always held passionately.

Bertrand Russell

Oratory

When I see a bird that walks like a duck, swims like a duck and quacks like a duck, I call that bird a duck.

Attributed to Richard Cardinal Cushing

Then there was a maiden speech, so inaudible, that it was doubted whether, after all, the young orator really did lose his virginity.

Benjamin Disraeli

It is amazing how soon one becomes accustomed to the sound of one's voice, when forced to repeat a speech five or six times a day. As election day approaches, the size of the crowds grows; they are more responsive and more interested; and one derives a certain exhilaration from that which, only a few weeks before, was intensely painful. This is one possible explanation of unlimited debate in the Senate.

J. William Fulbright

...I should consider the speeches of Livy, Sallust, and Tacitus, as pre-eminent specimens of logic, taste, and that sententious brevity which, using not a word to spare, leaves not a moment for inattention to the hearer. Amplification is the vice of modern oratory.

Thomas Jefferson

(asked about the time it took to prepare his speeches) ...It depends. If I am to speak ten minutes, I need a week for preparation; if fifteen minutes, three days; if half an hour, two days; if an hour, I am ready now.

Josephus Daniels

Order

To conceive order, to return to order, to realize order in oneself, around oneself, of oneself, this is aesthetic and moral beauty, ...

Henri Frédéric Amiel

He who every morning plans the transactions of the day, and follows out the plan, carries on a thread which will guide him through the labyrinth of the most busy life.

Hugh Blair

Past

One thing alone not even God can do,
To make undone whatever hath been done.

Aristotle

There must be what Mr. Gladstone many years ago called "a blessed act of oblivion." We must all turn our backs upon the horrors of the past. We must look to the future. We cannot afford to drag forward across the years that are to come the hatreds and revenges which have sprung from the injuries of the past.

Winston Churchill

The dogmas of the quiet past, are inadequate to the stormy present.

Abraham Lincoln

Our duty is to preserve what the past has had to for itself, and to say for ourselves what shall be true for the future.

Attributed to John Ruskin

Those who cannot remember the past are condemned to repeat it...

George Santayana

Whereof what's past is prologue, what to come
In yours and my discharge.

Shakespeare

How can we live without our lives? How will we know it's us without our past?

John Steinbeck

More and more Emerson recedes grandly into history, as the future he predicted becomes a past.

Robert Penn Warren

Patriotism

We would rather starve than sell our national honor.

Indira Gandhi

I only regret that I have but one life to lose for my country.

Nathan Hale

With earnest prayers to all my friends to cherish mutual good will, to promote harmony and conciliation, and above all things to let the love of our country soar above all minor passions, I tender you the assurance of my affectionate esteem and respect.

Thomas Jefferson

Patriotism is the last refuge of a scoundrel.

Samuel Johnson

Ask not what your country can do for you—ask what you can do for your country.

John F. Kennedy

True patriotism sometimes requires of men to act exactly contrary, at one period, to that which it does at another, and the motive which impels them—the desire to do right—is precisely the same.

Robert E. Lee

Whenever you hear a man speak of his love for his country it is a sign that he expects to be paid for it.

H. L. Mencken

Peace

Glory to God in the highest, and on earth peace, good will toward men.

Luke 2:14.

Peace

They have healed also the hurt of the daughter of my people slightly, saying, Peace, peace; when there is no peace.

Jeremiah 6:14.

At present the peace of the world has been preserved, not by statesmen, but by capitalists.

Benjamin Disraeli

Peace is an unstable equilibrium, which can be preserved only by acknowledged supremacy or equal power.

Will and Ariel Durant

I like to believe that people, in the long run, are going to do more to promote peace than our governments. Indeed, I think that people want peace so much that one of these days governments had better get out of the way and let them have it.

Dwight D. Eisenhower

Peace with all nations, and the right which that gives us with respect to all nations, are our objects.

Thomas Jefferson

The plain truth is the day is coming when no single nation, however powerful, can undertake by itself to keep the peace outside its own borders.

Robert S. Mcnamara

For peace is not mere absence of war, but is a virtue that springs from force of character.

Benedictus De Spinoza

Only a peace between equals can last. Only a peace the very principle of which is equality and a common participation in a common benefit.

Woodrow Wilson

People

There are people in our society who should be separated and discarded. I think it's one of the tendencies of the liberal community to feel that every person in a nation of over 200 million can be made into a productive citizen.

Spiro T. Agnew

Let them eat cake.

Attributed to Marie Antoinette

My plan cannot fail if the people are with us and we ought not to succeed unless we do have the people with us.

William Jennings Bryan

There are no uninteresting things, there are only uninterested people.

Gilbert Keith Chesterson

I am a child of the House of Commons. I was brought up in my father's house to believe in democracy. "Trust the people"—that was his message.

Winston Churchill

A sense of this necessity, and a submission to it, is to me a new and consolatory proof that wherever the people are well informed they can be trusted with their own government; that whenever things get so far wrong as to attract their notice, they may be relied on to set them to rights.

Thomas Jefferson

The Lord prefers commonlooking people. That is the reason he makes so many of them.

Attributed to Abraham Lincoln

People

No democracy has ever long survived the failure of its adherents to be ready to die for it... My own conviction is this, the people must either go on or go under.

David Lloyd George

I do not want the voice of the people shut out.

Huey Long

Where there is no vision, the people perish.

Proverbs 29:18.

People are not an interruption of our business. People are our business.

Walter E. Washington

In the last analysis, my fellow countrymen, as we in America would be the first to claim, a people are responsible for the acts of their government.

Woodrow Wilson

Perfection

The great aim of culture is the aim of setting ourselves to ascertain what perfection is and how to make it prevail.

Matthew Arnold

I never expect to see a perfect work from imperfect man.

Alexander Hamilton

No one can be perfectly free till all are free; no one can be perfectly moral till all are moral; no one can be perfectly happy till all are happy.

Herbert Spencer

We are all imperfect. We can not expect perfect government.

William Howard Taft

By his father he is English, by his mother he is American—to my mind the blend which makes the perfect man.

Mark Twain

Perseverance

Never give in, never give in, *never, never, never, never*—in nothing, great or small, large or petty— never give in except to convictions of honour and good sense.

Winston Churchill

Nothing in the World can take the place of persistence... Persistence and determination are omnipotent. The slogan "press on" has solved and always will solve the problems of the human race.

Attributed to Calvin Coolidge

If we face our tasks with the resolution to solve them, who shall say that anything is impossible.

Wilfred Grenfell

Philosophy

But there are some people, nevertheless—and I am one of them—who think that the most practical and important thing about a man is still his view of the universe.

G. K. Chesterton

The mystery of the beginning of all things is insoluble by us; and I for one must be content to remain an agnostic.

Charles Darwin

Policy

In a scheme of policy which is devised for a nation, we should not limit our views to its operation during a single year, or even for a short term of years. We should look at its operation for a considerable time, and in war as well as in peace.

Henry Clay

There is no such thing as a fixed policy, because policy like all organic entities is always in the making.
Attributed to Lord Salisbury

There is an eternal dispute between those who imagine the world to suit their policy, and those who correct their policy to suit the realities of.the world.
Attributed to Albert Sorel

The really basic thing in government is policy. Bad administration, to be sure, can destroy good policy, but good administration can never save bad policy.
Adlai E. Stevenson

Political Parties

It's a damned good thing to remember in politics to stick to your party and never attempt to buy the favor of your enemies at the expense of your friends.
Joseph G. Cannon

The two great political parties of the nation have existed for the purpose, each in accordance with its own principles, of undertaking to serve the interests of the whole nation. Their members of the Congress are chosen with that great end in view.

Calvin Coolidge

You cannot choose between party government and Parliamentary government. I say you can have no Parliamentary government if you have no party government; and therefore when gentlemen denounce party government, they strike at the scheme of government which, in my opinion, has made this country great, and which, I hope, will keep it great.

Benjamin Disraeli

The two parties which divide the state, the party of Conservatism and that of Innovation, are very old, and have disputed the possession of the world ever since it was made.

Ralph Waldo Emerson

...but he should strive to be always mindful of the fact that he serves his party best who serves the country best.

Rutherford B. Hayes

...when party and officeholder differ as to how the national interest is to be served, we must place first the responsibility we owe not to our party or even to our constituents but to our individual consciences.

John F. Kennedy

I have no Politics. I am for the Party that is out of Power, no matter which one it is.

Will Rogers

I don't care to be involved in the crash–landing unless I can be in on the take–off.

Harold Stassen

Now is the time for all good men to come to the aid of the party.

Author unknown

249

Politicians

Man is by nature a political animal.

Aristotle

Politician. An eel in the fundamental mud upon which the superstructure of organized society is reared. When he wriggles he mistakes the agitation of his tail for the trembling of the edifice. As compared with the statesman, he suffers the disadvantage of being alive.

Ambrose Bierce

[Politicians] are the same all over. They promise to build a bridge even where there is no river.

Nikita S. Khrushchev

I once said cynically of a politician, "He'll double-cross that bridge when he comes to it."

Oscar Levant

There is no such thing as a nonpolitical speech by a politician.

Richard M. Nixon

He has been called a mediocre man; but this is unwarranted flattery. He was a politician of monumental littleness.

Theodore Roosevelt

I was really too honest a man to be a politician and live.

Attributed to Socrates

I'm proud that I'm a politician. A politician is a man who understands government, and it takes a politician to run a government. A statesman is a politician who's been dead 10 or 15 years.

Harry S Truman

I think politicians and movie actors and movie executives are similar in more ways than they're different.
There is an egocentric quality about both; there is a
very sensitive awareness of the public attitude... And
in a strange and bizarre way, when movie actors come
to Washington, they're absolutely fascinated by the
politicians. And when the politicians go to Hollywood,
they're absolutely fascinated by the movie stars. It's a
kind of reciprocity of affection by people who both recognize in a sense they're in the same racket.

Jack Valenti

I'm not a politician and my other habits are good. I've
no enemys to reward, nor friends to sponge. But I'm a
Union man.

Artemus Ward

I'd rather keep my promises to other politicians than
to God. God, at least, has a degree of forgiveness.

Author unknown

Politics

Practical politics consists in ignoring facts.

Henry Adams

People who think the mighty in Washington can be
persuaded, or corrupted, if you will, by anything less
than votes just don't understand what it's all about
and never will. They don't know what Washington
juice is made of.

George E. Allen

Push. One of the two things mainly conducive to success, especially in politics. The other is Pull.

Ambrose Bierce

Politics

Politics is the art of the possible.

Otto Von Bismarck

A political career brings out the basest qualities in human nature.

Lord Bryce

Politics ought to be the part-time profession of every citizen who would protect the rights and privileges of free people and who would preserve what is good and fruitful in our national heritage.

Dwight D. Eisenhower

The whole aim of practical politics is to keep the populace alarmed (and hence clamorous to be led to safety) by menacing it with an endless series of hobgoblins, all of them imaginary.

H. L. Mencken

The whole art of politics consists in directing rationally the irrationalities of men.

Reinhold Niebuhr

They are wrong who think that politics is like an ocean voyage or a military campaign, something to be done with some particular end in view, something which leaves off as soon as that end is reached. It is not a public chore, to be got over with. It is a way of life.

Attributed to Plutarch

The most practical kind of politics is the politics of decency.

Theodore Roosevelt

Politics is perhaps the only profession for which no preparation is thought necessary.

Robert Louis Stevenson

There is hardly a political question in the United States which does not sooner or later turn into a judicial one.

Alexis de Tocqueville

Politics is a fascinating game, because politics is government. It is the art of government.

Harry S Truman

Politics makes strange bedfellows.

Charles Dudley Warner

Until you've been in politics you've never really been alive. It's rough and sometimes it's dirty and it's always hard work and tedious details. But, it's the only sport for grownups—all other games are for kids.

Author unknown.

Positive Thinking

For myself I am an optimist—it does not seem to be much use being anything else.

Winston Churchill

Keep your face to the sunshine and you cannot see the shadow.

Helen Keller

If you think you are beaten, you are;
If you think you dare not, you don't.
If you'd like to win, but think you can't,
It's almost a cinch you won't.
If you think you'll lose, you're lost,
For out in the world we find
Success begins with a fellow's will;
It's all in the state of mind.

Walter D. Wintle

Poverty

This administration today, here and now, declares unconditional war on poverty...

Lyndon B. Johnson

It is easy enough to tell the poor to accept their poverty as God's will when you yourself have warm clothes and plenty of food and medical care and a roof over your head and no worry about the rent. But if you want them to believe you—try to share some of their poverty and see if you can accept it as God's will yourself.

Thomas Merton

The poor in Resurrection City have come to Washington to show that the poor in America are sick, dirty, disorganized, and powerless—and they are criticized daily for being sick, dirty, disorganized, and powerless.

Calvin Trillin

Power

Power tends to corrupt and absolute power corrupts absolutely. Great men are almost always bad men, even when they exercise influence and not authority: still more when you superadd the tendency or the certainty of corruption by authority.

Lord Acton

...our politics has failed. Since no politician can afford to admit this, we must pretend that we are resorting to power in order to make our politics succeed.

Theodore Draper

In the main it will be found that a power over a man's support is a power over his will.

Alexander Hamilton

There are similarities between absolute power and absolute faith: a demand for absolute obedience, a readiness to attempt the impossible, a bias for simple solutions—to cut the knot rather than unravel it, the viewing of compromise as surrender. Both absolute power and absolute faith are instruments of dehumanization. Hence, absolute faith corrupts as absolutely as absolute power.

Eric Hoffer

The essence of Government is power; and power, lodged as it must be in human hands, will ever be liable to abuse.

James Madison

...I believe there are more instances of the abridgment of the freedom of the people, by gradual and silent encroachments of those in power, than by violent and sudden usurpations.

James Madison

Beware of the man who rises to power
From one suspender.

Edgar Lee Masters

The power of Kings and Magistrates is nothing else, but what is only derivative, transferr'd and committed to them in trust from the People, to the Common good of them all, in whom the power yet remaines fundamentally, and cannot be tak'n from them, without a violation of thir natural birthright.

John Milton

Power

When I resist, therefore, ... the concentration of power, I am resisting the processes of death, because the concentration of power is what always precedes the destruction of human initiative, and, therefore of human energy.

Woodrow Wilson

Praise

Praise from the common people is generally false, and rather follows the vain than the virtuous.

Francis Bacon

It is not for minds like ours to give or to receive flattery; yet the praises of sincerity have ever been permitted to the voice of friendship.

George Gordon, Lord Byron

I am about courting a girl I have had but little acquaintance with. How shall I come to a knowledge of her faults, and whether she has the virtues I imagine she has? *Answer.* Commend her among her female acquaintance.

Benjamin Franklin

He who praises everybody, praises nobody.

Attributed to Samuel Johnson

Prayer

Grant us a common faith that man shall know bread and peace—that he shall know justice and righteousness, freedom and security, an equal opportunity and an equal chance to do his best not only in our own lands, but throughout the world.

Stephen Vincent Benét

God give me the serenity to accept
    things which cannot be changed;
Give me courage to change
    things which must be changed;
And the wisdom to distinguish one from the other.
Attributed to Reinhold Niebuhr

Common people do not pray; they only beg.
George Bernard Shaw

May the road rise to meet you,
May the wind be always at your back,
May the sun shine warm upon your face,
May the rain fall soft upon your fields,
And, until we meet again,
May God hold you in the palm of His hand.
Author unknown

Prejudice

To hate a man because he was born in another country, because he speaks a different language, or because he takes a different view on this subject or that, is a great folly.
Attributed to Johann Amos Comenius

Prejudices are rarely overcome by argument; not being founded in reason they cannot be destroyed by logic.
Tryon Edwards

Whoever seeks to set one nationality against another, seeks to degrade all nationalities. Whoever seeks to set one race against another seeks to enslave all races. Whoever seeks to set one religion against another, seeks to destroy all religion.
Franklin D. Roosevelt

Prejudice

Sex prejudice is so ingrained in our society that many who practice it are simply unaware that they are hurting women. *It is the last socially acceptable prejudice.*

Bernice Sandler

Presidency

President. The leading figure in a small group of men of whom—and of whom only—it is positively known that immense numbers of their countrymen did not want any of them for President.

Ambrose Bierce

And still the question, "What shall be done with our ex–Presidents?" is not laid at rest; and I sometimes think Watterson's solution of it, "Take them out and shoot them," is worthy of attention.

Grover Cleveland

The second office of this government is honorable & easy, the first is but a splendid misery.

Thomas Jefferson

You have heard the story, haven't you, about the man who was tarred and feathered and carried out of town on a rail? A man in the crowd asked him how he liked it. His reply was that if it was not for the honor of the thing, he would much rather walk.

Abraham Lincoln

Americans have a love for the President that goes beyond loyalty or party nationality; he is ours, and we exercise the right to destroy him.

John Steinbeck

Press

To the press alone, chequered as it is with abuses, the world is indebted for all the triumphs which have been gained by reason and humanity over error and oppression.

James Madison

Whenever the press quits abusing me I know I'm in the wrong pew.

Harry S. Truman

In America the President reigns for four years, and Journalism governs for ever and ever.

Oscar Wilde

Prisons

Nothing can be more abhorrent to democracy than to imprison a person or keep him in prison because he is unpopular. This is really the test of civilisation.

Winston Churchill

A prison taint was on everything there. The imprisoned air, the imprisoned light, the imprisoned damps, the imprisoned men, were all deteriorated by confinement. As the captive men were faded and haggard, so the iron was rusty, the stone was slimy, the wood was rotten, the air was faint, the light was dim. Like a well, like a vault, like a tomb, the prison had no knowledge of the brightness outside; ...

Charles Dickens

The degree of civilization in a society can be judged by entering its prisons.

Attributed to Fyodor Dostoevsky

Privacy

We are rapidly entering the age of no privacy, where everyone is open to surveillance at all times; where there are no secrets from government.
William O. Douglas

Every man should know that his conversations, his correspondence, and his personal life are private.
Lyndon B. Johnson

Gentlemen do not read each other's mail.
Henry L. Stimson

Progress

A journey of a thousand miles must begin with a single step.

Chinese proverb

The advancement of the arts from year to year taxes our credulity, and seems to presage the arrival of that period when human improvement must end.
Henry L. Ellsworth

I walk slowly, but I never walk backward.
Attributed to Abraham Lincoln

I hope to 'stand firm' enough to not go backward, and yet not go forward fast enough to wreck the country's cause.

Attributed to Abraham Lincoln

The chief cause which made the fusion of the different elements of society so imperfect was the extreme difficulty which our ancestors found in passing from place to place.

Thomas Babington Macaulay

Expositions are the timekeepers of progress.

William McKinley

Two conditions render difficult this historic situation of mankind: It is full of tremendously deadly armament, and it has not progressed morally as much as it has scientifically and technically.

Pope Paul VI

I was to learn later in life that we tend to meet any new situation by reorganizing, and a wonderful method it can be for creating the illusion of progress while producing confusion, inefficiency, and demoralization.

Attributed to Petronius Arbiter

Our inventions are wont to be pretty toys, which distract our attention from serious things. They are but improved means to an unimproved end... We are in great haste to construct a magnetic telegraph from Maine to Texas; but Maine and Texas, it may be, have nothing important to communicate.

Henry David Thoreau

The day of large profits is probably past. There may be room for further intensive, but not extensive, development of industry in the present area of civilization.

D. Carroll Wright

Promises

If you make a promise, the thing is still uncertain, depends on a future day, and concerns but few people; but if you refuse you alienate people to a certainty and at once, and many people too.

Cicero

Promises

We must not promise what we ought not, lest we be called on to perform what we cannot.

Attributed to Abraham Lincoln

The Great Spirit placed me and my people on this land poor and naked. When the white men came we gave them lands, and did not wish to hurt them. But the white man drove us back and took our lands. Then the Great Father made us many promises, but they are not kept. He promised to give us large presents, and when they came to us they were small; ...

Sioux Indian Chief Red Cloud

Promises and Pye–Crusts, ... are made to be broken.

Jonathan Swift

Property

Property is the fruit of labor—property is desirable—is a positive good in the world. That some should be rich shows that others may become rich, and hence is just encouragement to industry and enterprize. Let not him who is houseless pull down the house of another; but let him labor diligently and build one for himself, thus by example assuring that his own shall be safe from violence when built.

Abraham Lincoln

As a man is said to have a right to his property, he may be equally said to have a property in his rights.

James Madison

Give a man the secure possession of a bleak rock, and he will turn it into a garden; give him a nine years lease of a garden, and he will convert it into a desert... The magic of *property* turns sand to gold.

Arthur Young

Public Affairs

My rule, in which I have always found satisfaction, is, never to turn aside in public affairs through views of private interest; but to go straight forward in doing what appears to me right at the time, leaving the consequences with Providence.

Benjamin Franklin

An Athenian citizen does not neglect the state because he takes care of his own household; and even those of us who are engaged in business have a very fair idea of politics. We alone regard a man who takes no interest in public affairs, not as a harmless, but as a useless character, and if few of us are originators, we are all sound judges of a policy.

Thucydides

Public Opinion

...today, we have more than our share of the nattering nabobs of negativism. They have formed their own 4-H Club-the "hopeless, hysterical hyponchondriacs of history."

Spiro T. Agnew

Nothing is more dangerous in wartime than to live in the temperamental atmosphere of a Gallup Poll, always feeling one's pulse and taking one's temperature. I see that a speaker at the weekend said that this was a time when leaders should keep their ears to the ground. All I can say is that the British nation will find it very hard to look up to leaders who are detected in that somewhat ungainly posture.

Winston Churchill

Public Opinion

I had grown tired of standing in the lean and lonely
front line facing the greatest enemy that ever con-
fronted man—public opinion.

Clarence Darrow

Heroes are created by popular demand, sometimes out
of the scantiest materials, or none at all.

Gerald W. Johnson

In this and like communities, public sentiment is everything. With public sentiment, nothing can fail; without it nothing can succeed.

Abraham Lincoln

Private opinion creates public opinion. Public opinion
overflows eventually into national behaviour and national behaviour, as things are arranged at present,
can make or mar the world. That is why private opinion, and private behaviour, and private conversation
are so terrifyingly important.

Jan Struther

Public Service

We must not in the course of public life expect immediate approbation and immediate grateful acknowl-
edgment of our services. But let us persevere through
abuse and even injury. The internal satisfaction of a
good conscience is always present, and time will do us
justice in the minds of the people, even those at present the most prejudiced against us.

Benjamin Franklin

...every kind of service necessary for the public good,
becomes honorable by being necessary.

Captain Nathan Hale

When a man assumes a public trust, he should consider himself as public property.

Attributed to Thomas Jefferson

A private Life is to be preferr'd; the Honour and Gain of publick Posts, bearing no proportion with the Comfort of it.

William Penn

...if you are too timid or too fastidious or too careless to do your part in this work, then you forfeit your right to be considered one of the governing and you become one of the governed instead—one of the driven cattle of the political arena.

Theodore Roosevelt

There is no idea so uplifting as the idea of the service of humanity.

Woodrow Wilson

The office should seek the man, not man the office.

Attributed to Silas Wright

Publicity

Publicity is justly commended as a remedy for social and industrial diseases. Sunlight is said to be the best of disinfectants; electric light the most efficient policeman.

Louis D. Brandeis

The government being the people's business, it necessarily follows that its operations should be at all times open to the public view. Publicity is therefore as essential to honest administration as freedom of speech is to representative government.

William Jennings Bryan

Reason

A crowd always thinks with its sympathy, never with its reason.

William Alger

Ethics make one's soul mannerly and wise, but logic is the armory of reason, furnished with all offensive and defensive weapons.

Thomas Fuller

A man always has two reasons for what he does—a good one, and the real one.

Attributed to J. Pierpont Morgan

Reform

A rayformer thinks he was ilicted because he was a rayformer, whin th' thruth iv th' matther is he was ilicted because no wan knew him.

Finley Peter Dunne

The voice of great events is proclaiming to us, Reform, that you may preserve.

Thomas Babington Macaulay

The best reformers the world has ever seen are those who commence on themselves.

Attributed to George Bernard Shaw

Regulation

No rule is so general,
      which admits not some exception.

Robert Burton

The general rule, at least, is that while property may be regulated to a certain extent, if regulation goes too far it will be recognized as a taking.

Oliver Wendell Holmes

It is hardly lack of due process for the Government to regulate that which it subsidizes.

Robert H. Jackson

Every system should allow loopholes and exceptions, for if it does not it will in the end crush all that is best in man.

Bertrand Russell

Will one of you gentlemen tell me in what civilized country of the earth there are important government boards of control on which private interests are represented? Which of you gentlemen thinks the railroads should select members of the Interstate Commerce Commission?

Attributed to Woodrow Wilson

Republic

The Republic needed to be passed through chastening, purifying fires of adversity and suffering: so these came and did their work and the verdure of a new national life springs greenly, luxuriantly, from their ashes.

Horace Greeley

But every difference of opinion is not a difference of principle. We have called by different names brethren of the same principle. We are all republicans—we are federalists.

Thomas Jefferson

Responsibility

A hundred times every day I remind myself that my inner and outer life are based on the labors of other men, living and dead, and that I must exert myself in order to give in the same measure as I have received and am still receiving.

Albert Einstein

If I knew something useful to me and harmful to my family, I should put it out of my mind. If I knew something useful to my family and not to my country, I should try to forget it. If I knew something useful to my country and harmful to Europe, or useful to Europe and harmful to the human race, I should consider it a crime.

Montesquieu

There is a mysterious cycle in human events. To some generations much is given. Of other generations much is expected.

Franklin D. Roosevelt

(The earth) belongs as much to those who are to come after us, and whose names are already written in the book of creation, as to us; and we have no right, by anything that we do or neglect, to involve them in unnecessary penalties, or deprive them of benefits which it was in our power to bequeath.

John Ruskin

The eyes of all people are upon us. Soe that if we shall deal falsely with our God in this work we have undertaken, and so cause him to withdraw his present help from us, we shall be made a story and a byword throughout the world.

John Winthrop

Revolution

...I am proud this morning to salute you as fellow revolutionaries. Neither you nor I are willing to accept the tyranny of poverty, nor the dictatorship of ignorance, nor the despotism of ill health, nor the oppression of bias and prejudice and bigotry. We want change. We want progress. We want it both abroad and at home—and we aim to get it.

Lyndon B. Johnson

Those who make peaceful revolution impossible will make violent revolution inevitable.

John F. Kennedy

...we live in an era of revolution—the revolution of rising expectations.

Adlai E. Stevenson

Rich

Riches are for spending, and spending for honor and good actions; therefore extraordinary expense must be limited by the worth of the occasion.

Francis Bacon

"I was told," continued Egremont, "that an impassable gulf divided the Rich from the Poor; I was told that the Privileged and the People formed Two Nations, governed by different laws, influenced by different manners, with no thoughts or sympathies in common; with an innate inability of mutual comprehension."

Benjamin Disraeli

This country cannot afford to be materially rich and spiritually poor.

John F. Kennedy

Rich

I take it that it is best for all to leave each man free to acquire property as fast as he can. Some will get wealthy. I don't believe in a law to prevent a man from getting rich; it would do more harm than good.

Abraham Lincoln

Right

Still, if you will not fight for the right when you can easily win without bloodshed; if you will not fight when your victory will be sure and not too costly; you may come to the moment when you will have to fight with all the odds against you and only a precarious chance of survival. There may even be a worse case. You may have to fight when there is no hope of victory, because it is better to perish than live as slaves.

Winston Churchill

To see what is right and not to do it is want of courage.

Confucius

You may burn my body to ashes, and scatter them to the winds of heaven; you may drag my soul down to the regions of darkness and despair to be tormented forever; but you will never get me to support a measure which I believe to be wrong, although by doing so I may accomplish that which I believe to be right.

Attributed to Abraham Lincoln

Stand with anybody that stands *right*. Stand with him while he is right and *part* with him when he goes wrong.

Abraham Lincoln

Let us not be content to wait and see what will happen, but give us the determination to make the right things happen.

Peter Marshall

Nothing is politically right which is morally wrong.

Attributed to Daniel O'connell

Aggressive fighting for the right is the noblest sport the world affords.

Theodore Roosevelt

My country, right or wrong; if right, to be kept right; and if wrong, to be set right.

Carl Schurz

The greatest right in the world is the right to be wrong.

Harry Weinberger

Science

Logic and metaphysics make use of more tools than all the rest of the sciences put together, and they do the least work.

Charles Caleb Colton

Science without religion is lame, religion without science is blind.

Albert Einstein

We give the name scientist to the type of man who has felt experiment to be a means guiding him to search out the deep truth of life, to lift a veil from its fascinating secrets, and who, in this pursuit, has felt arising within him a love for the mysteries of nature, so passionate as to annihilate the thought of himself.

Maria Montessori

Science

A new scientific truth does not triumph by convincing its opponents and making them see the light, but rather because its opponents eventually die, and a new generation grows up that is familiar with it.

Max Planck

Sea

I have seen the sea lashed into fury and tossed into spray, and its grandeur moves the soul of the dullest man; but I remember that it is not the billows, but the calm level of the sea from which all heights and depths are measured.

James A. Garfield

As they say... a rising tide lifts all the boats. And a partnership, by definition, serves both partners, without domination or unfair advantage.

John F. Kennedy

Self

Nothing is easier than self-deceit. For what each man wishes, that he also believes to be true.

Demosthenes

I now know all the people worth knowing in America, and I find no intellect comparable to my own.

Margaret Fuller

The compulsion to take ourselves seriously is in inverse proportion to our creative capacity. When the creative flow dries up, all we have left is our importance.

Eric Hoffer

...if at the end I have lost every other friend on earth I shall at least have one friend remaining and that one shall be down inside me.

Attributed to Abraham Lincoln

This above all: to thine own self be true,
And it must follow, as the night the day,
Thou canst not then be false to any man.

Shakespeare

What we do belongs to what we are; and what we are is what becomes of us.

Henry Van Dyke

Sex

I don't see why we can't get along just as well with a polygamist who doesn't polyg as we do with a lot of monogamists who don't monog!

Attributed to Boies Penrose

I lose my respect for the man who can make the mystery of sex the subject of a coarse jest, yet when you speak earnestly and seriously on the subject, is silent.

Henry David Thoreau

The state has no business in the bedrooms of the nation.

Pierre Trudeau

Ships

It is cheering to see that the rats are still around—the ship is not sinking.

Eric Hoffer

Ships

[A ship is always referred to as "she"] ...because it costs so much to keep one in paint and powder.

Rear Admiral Chester W. Nimitz

Silence

In some causes silence is dangerous; so if any know of conspiracies against their country or king, or any that might greatly prejudice their neighbor, they ought to discover it.

Attributed to St. Ambrose

Under all speech that is good for anything there lies a silence that is better. Silence is deep as Eternity; speech is shallow as Time.

Thomas Carlyle

Blessed is the man who, having nothing to say, abstains from giving us wordy evidence of the fact.

George Eliot

We will have to repent in this generation not merely for the vitriolic words and actions of the bad people, but for the appalling silence of the good people.

Martin Luther King, Jr.

Great souls endure in silence.

Friedrich Schiller

Silence is the perfectest herald of joy:
I were but little happy if I could say how much.

Shakespeare

Slavery

But this is slavery, not to speak one's thought.

Euripides

Whenever [I] hear any one arguing for slavery I feel a strong impulse to see it tried on him personally.

Abraham Lincoln

All socialism involves slavery... That which fundamentally distinguishes the slave is that he labours under coercion to satisfy another's desires.

Herbert Spencer

Not only do I pray for it, on the score of human dignity, but I can clearly forsee that nothing but the rooting out of slavery can perpetuate the existence of our union, by consolidating it in a common bond of principle.

Attributed to George Washington

Sleep

"Laugh and the world laughs with you, snore and you sleep alone."

Mrs. Patrick Campbell

If you would relish food, labor for it before you take it; if you enjoy clothing, pay for it before you wear it; if you would sleep soundly, take a clear conscience to bed with you.

Benjamin Franklin

Society

Now the vicissitudes that afflict the individual have their source in society. ... Personal relations have given way to impersonal ones. The Great Society has arrived and the task of our generation is to bring it under control.

Aneurin Bevan

Society

[Society] is a partnership in all science, a partnership in all art, a partnership in every virtue and in all perfection. As the ends of such a partnership cannot be obtained in many generations, it becomes a partnership not only between those who are living, but between those who are living, those who are dead, and those who are to be born.

Edmund Burke

We must beware of trying to build a society in which nobody counts for anything except a politician or an official, a society where enterprise gains no reward and thrift no privileges.

Winston Churchill

The nature of a society is largely determined by the direction in which talent and ambition flow–by the tilt of the social landscape.

Eric Hoffer

The principles of Jefferson are the definitions and axioms of free society.

Abraham Lincoln

Soldiers

...unless one values the lives of his soldiers and is tormented by their ordeal he is unfit to command.

Omar Nelson Bradley

If I should die, think only this of me:
That there's some corner of a foreign field
That is forever England.

Rupert Brooke

The patriot volunteer, fighting for country and his rights, makes the most reliable soldier on earth.

Attributed to Stonewall Jackson

Honor to the Soldier, and Sailor everywhere, who bravely bears his country's cause. Honor also to the citizen who cares for his brother in the field, and serves, as he best can, the same cause—honor to him, only less than to him, who braves, for the common good, the storms of heaven and the storms of battle.

Abraham Lincoln

...it has been said, all that a man hath will he give for his life; and while all contribute of their substance the soldier puts his life at stake, and often yields it up in his country's cause. The highest merit, then, is due to the soldier.

Abraham Lincoln

Old soldiers never die; they just fade away.

General Douglas Macarthur

The soldier, above all other men, is required to perform the highest act of religious teaching—sacrifice. In battle and in the face of danger and death he discloses those divine attributes which his Maker gave when He created man in his own image. No physical courage and no brute instincts can take the place of the divine annunciation and spiritual uplift which will alone sustain him.

General Douglas Macarthur

It is foolish and wrong to mourn the men who died. Rather we should thank God that such men lived.

Attributed to General George S. Patton

Soldiers

Our *God* and *Souldiers* we alike adore,
Ev'n at the Brink of danger; not before:
After deliverance, both alike required;
Our *God's* forgotten, and our *Souldiers* slighted.
Francis Quarles

So, as you go into battle, remember your ancestors and remember your descendants.
Tacitus

These endured all and gave all that justice among nations might prevail and that mankind might enjoy freedom and inherit peace.
Author Unknown

Solution

There is always an easy solution to every human problem—neat, plausible, and wrong.
H. L. Mencken

Space

The emergence of this new world poses a vital issue: will outer space be preserved for peaceful use and developed for the benefit of all mankind? Or will it become another focus for the arms race—and thus an area of dangerous and sterile competition? The choice is urgent. And it is ours to make.
Dwight D. Eisenhower

...Well, space is there, and we're going to climb it, and the moon and the planets are there, and new hopes for knowledge and peace are there.
John F. Kennedy

To see the earth as we now see it, small and blue and beautiful in that eternal silence where it floats, is to see ourselves as riders on the earth together, brothers on that bright loveliness in the unending night—brothers who see now they are truly brothers.

Archibald Macleish

Some say God is living [in space]. I was looking around very attentively, but I did not see anyone there. I did not detect either angels or gods . . . I don't believe in God. I believe in man—his strength, his possibilities, his reason.

Gherman Titov

Speaking Out

Discretion in speech, is more than eloquence.

Francis Bacon

...Why, if any of you young gentlemen have a mind to get heard a mile off, you must make a bonfire of your reputation, and a close enemy of most men who wish you well. And what will you get in return? Well, if I must for the benefit of the economists, charge you up with some selfish gain, I will say that you get the satisfaction of having been heard, and that this is the whole possible scope of human ambition.

John Jay Chapman

Least said, soonest mended.

Charles Dickens

Without Freedom of Thought, there can be no such Thing as Wisdom; and no such Thing as publick Liberty, without Freedom of Speech.

Benjamin Franklin

Speaking Out

Every absurdity has a champion to defend it, for error is always talkative.

Oliver Goldsmith

Be swift to hear, slow to speak, slow to wrath.

James 1:19

Every time we turn our heads the other way when we see the law flouted—when we tolerate what we know to be wrong—when we close our eyes and ears to the corrupt because we are too busy, or too frightened—when we fail to speak up and speak out—we strike a blow against freedom and decency and justice.

Robert F. Kennedy

Singular indeed that the people should be writhing under oppression and injury, and yet not one among them to be found, to raise the voice of complaint.

Abraham Lincoln

Debate is the death of conversation.

Emil Ludwig

When Hitler attacked the Jews ... I was not a Jew, therefore, I was not concerned. And when Hitler attacked the Catholics, I was not a Catholic, and therefore, I was not concerned. And when Hitler attacked the unions and the industrialists, I was not a member of the unions and I was not concerned. Then, Hitler attacked me and the Protestant church—and there was nobody left to be concerned.

Attributed to Martin Niemöller

Nature has given us two ears, two eyes, and but one tongue, to the end that we should hear and see more than we speak.

Socrates

He knows not when to be silent who knows not when to speak.

Publilius Syrus

Spending

Nothing is easier than spending the public money. It does not appear to belong to anybody. The temptation is overwhelming to bestow it on somebody.

Attributed to Calvin Coolidge

A billion here, a billion there, and pretty soon you're talking about real money.

Attributed to Senator Everett M. Dirksen

That most delicious of all privileges—spending other people's money.

John Randolph of Roanoke

Lord, the money we do spend on Government and it's not one bit better than the government we got for one-third the money twenty years ago.

Will Rogers

Spirit

The sword conquered for a while, but the spirit conquers for ever!

Sholem Asch

If that vital spark that we find in a grain of wheat can pass unchanged through countless deaths and resurrections, will the spirit of man be unable to pass from this body to another?

William Jennings Bryan

281

Spirit

I am certain that after the dust of centuries has passed over our cities, we, too, will be remembered not for victories or defeats in battle or in politics, but for our contribution to the human spirit.

John F. Kennedy

Glendower: I can call spirits from the vasty deep.
Hotspur: Why, so can I, or so can any man;
    But will they come when you do call for them?

Shakespeare

State

It is one of the happy incidents of the federal system that a single courageous State may, if its citizens choose, serve as a laboratory; and try novel social and economic experiments without risk to the rest of the country.

Louis D. Brandeis

We are gong down the road to stateism. Where we will wind up, no one can tell, but if some of the new programs seriously proposed should be adopted, there is danger that the individual—whether farmer, worker, manufacturer, lawyer, or doctor—will soon be an economic slave pulling an oar in the galley of the state.

James F. Byrnes

The first act by virtue of which the State really constitutes itself the representative of the whole of society— the taking possession of the means of production in the name of society—this is, at the same time, its last independent act as a State.

Friedrich Engels

...a State cannot be expected to move with the celerity of a private business man; it is enough if it proceeds, in the language of the English Chancery, with all deliberate speed.

Oliver Wendell Holmes

The church must be reminded that it is not the master or the servant of the state but rather the conscience of the state.

Martin Luther King, Jr.

Statesman

When statesmen forsake their own private conscience for the sake of their public duties... they lead their country by a short route to chaos.

Robert Bolt

A disposition to preserve, and an ability to improve, taken together, would be my standard of a statesman. Everything else is vulgar in the conception, perilous in the execution.

Edmund Burke

A great statesman is he who knows when to depart from traditions, as well as when to adhere to them.

John Stuart Mill

Statesmen have to bend to the collective will of their peoples or be broken.

Attributed to Woodrow Wilson

Statistics

The individual source of the statistics may easily be the weakest link.

Josiah Stamp

Statistics

There are three kinds of lies: lies, damned lies, and statistics.

Mark Twain

Strength

Our real problem, then, is not our strength today; it is rather the vital necessity of action today to ensure our strength tomorrow.

Dwight D. Eisenhower

We all have enough strength to endure the misfortunes of others.

François De La Rochefoucauld

It is from weakness that people reach for dictators and concentrated government power. Only the strong can be free. And only the productive can be strong.

Wendell Willkie

Strike

There is no right to strike against the public safety by anybody anywhere, anytime.

Calvin Coolidge

I am glad to know that there is a system of labor where the laborer can strike if he wants to! I would to God that such a system prevailed all over the world.

Abraham Lincoln

Success

The road to success is filled with women pushing their husbands along.

Attributed to Lord Thomas R. Dewar

I have climbed to the top of the greasy pole!
Benjamin Disraeli

The secret of success is constancy of purpose.
Benjamin Disraeli

If a man can write a better book, preach a better sermon, or make a better mousetrap than his neighbor, ... the world will make a beaten path to his door.
Attributed to Ralph Waldo Emerson

But I like not these great successes of yours; for I know how jealous are the gods.
Herodotus

Even on the most exalted throne in the world we are only sitting on our own bottom.
Michel Eyquem de Montaigne

There is only one success ... to be able to spend your life in your own way, and not to give others absurd maddening claims upon it.
Christopher Morley

Success is the necessary misfortune of life, but it is only to the very unfortunate that it comes early.
Anthony Trollope

We must walk consciously only part way toward our goal, and then leap in the dark to our success.
Attributed to Henry David Thoreau

Taxation

To please universally was the object of his life; but to tax and to please, no more than to love and to be wise, is not given to men.
Edmund Burke

Taxation

The art of taxation consists in so plucking the goose as to obtain the largest possible amount of feathers with the smallest possible amount of hissing.

Attributed to Jean Baptiste Colbert

Of all debts men are least willing to pay the taxes. What a satire is this on government! Everywhere they think they get their money's worth, except for these.

Ralph Waldo Emerson

We shall tax and tax, and spend and spend, and elect and elect.

Attributed to Harry L. Hopkins

A government which robs Peter to pay Paul can always depend on the support of Paul.

George Bernard Shaw

In other words, a democratic government is the only one in which those who vote for a tax can escape the obligation to pay it.

Alexis de Tocqueville

Teaching

Teachers who educated children deserved more honour than parents who merely gave them birth; for bare life is furnished by the one, the other ensures a good life.

Attributed to Aristotle

Give a man a fish and you feed him for a day. Teach a man to fish and you feed him for a lifetime.

Chinese proverb

Who dares to teach must never cease to learn.

John Cotton Dana

The whole art of teaching is only the art of awakening the natural curiosity of young minds for the purpose of satisfying it afterwards; and curiosity itself can be vivid and wholesome only in proportion as the mind is contented and happy.

Anatole France

He who can, does. He who cannot, teaches.

George Bernard Shaw

Television

I invite you to sit down in front of your television set when your station goes on the air... and keep your eyes glued to that set until the station signs off. I can assure you that you will observe a vast wasteland.

Newton N. Minow

Unless and until there is unmistakable proof to the contrary, the presumption must be that television is and will be a main factor in influencing the values and moral standards of our society...

Pilkington Report

Those who say they give the public what it wants begin by underestimating public taste, and end by debauching it.

Pilkington Report

Thought

If a man take no thought about what is distant, he will find sorrow near at hand.

Confucius

No brain is stronger than its weakest think.

Thomas L. Masson

Thought

To him whose elastic and vigorous thought keeps pace
with the sun, the day is a perpetual morning.

Henry David Thoreau

Time

To every thing there is a season,
   and time to every purpose under the heaven:
A time to be born, and a time to die;
  a time to plant, and a time to pluck up
      that which is planted;
A time to kill, and a time to heal;
  a time to break down, and a time to build up;
A time to weep, and a time to laugh;
  a time to mourn, and a time to dance;
A time to cast away stones, and a time to
      gather stones together;
  a time to embrace, and a time to refrain
      from embracing;
A time to get, and a time to lose;
  a time to keep, and a time to cast away;
A time to rend, and a time to sew;
  a time to keep silence, and a time to speak;
A time to love, and a time to hate;
  a time of war, and a time of peace.

Ecclesiastes 3:1–8

"The time has come," the Walrus said,
"To talk of many things:
Of shoes—and ships—and sealing wax—
Of cabbages—and kings—
And why the sea is boiling hot—
And whether pigs have wings."

Lewis Carroll

One always has time enough, if one will apply it well.
Johann Wolfgang Von Goethe

There is no time like the old time,
>   when you and I were young,
When the buds of April blossomed,
>   and the birds of spring–time sung!
The garden's brightest glories
>   by summer suns are nursed,
But oh, the sweet, sweet violets,
>   the flowers that opened first!
Oliver Wendell Holmes

Time is at once the most valuable and the most perishable of all our possessions.
John Randolph of Roanoke

The opera ain't over till the fat lady sings.
Dan Cook

Times

It was the best of times, it was the worst of times, it was the age of wisdom, it was the age of foolishness, it was the epoch of belief, it was the epoch of incredulity, it was the season of Light, it was the season of Darkness, it was the spring of hope, it was the winter of despair, we had everything before us, we had nothing before us, we were all going direct to Heaven, we were all going direct the other way—in short, the period was so far like the present period, that some of its noisiest authorities insisted on its being received, for good or for evil, in the superlative degree of comparison only.

Charles Dickens

These times of ours are serious and full of calamity, but all times are essentially alike. As soon as there is life there is danger.

Ralph Waldo Emerson

This time, like all times, is a very good one, if we but know what to do with it.

Ralph Waldo Emerson

These are the times that try men's souls. The summer soldier and the sunshine patriot will, in this crisis, shrink from the service of their country; but he that stands it now, deserves the love and thanks of man and woman.

Thomas Paine

The man and the hour have met.

William Yancey

Timing

On the Plains of Hesitation bleach the bones of countless millions who, at the Dawn of Victory, sat down to wait, and waiting—died!

George W. Cecil

A clear strong statement of a case if made too soon or too late fails. If well made at the right time it is effective. It is a nice point to study the right time.

James A. Garfield

Treason

Treason doth never prosper, what's the reason?
For if it prosper, none dare call it Treason.

John Harington

Trust

Trust men and they will be true to you; treat them greatly and they will show themselves great.

Ralph Waldo Emerson

Preserve me, 0 God: for in thee do I put my trust.

Psalms 16:1.

We have a saying in the movement that we don't trust anybody over 30.

Jack Weinberg

Truth

The truth is often a terrible weapon of aggression. It is possible to lie, and even to murder, with the truth.

Alfred Adler

Truth, crushed to earth, shall rise again;
Th' eternal years of God are hers;
But Error, wounded, writhes in pain,
And dies among his worshippers.

William Cullen Bryant

With a man, a lie is a last resort; with women, it's First Aid.

Frank Burgess

Hell is truth seen too late—duty neglected in its season.

Attributed to Tryon Edwards

I believe that truth is the glue that holds government together not only our Movement but civilization itself. That bond, though strained, is unbroken at home and abroad.

Gerald R. Ford

Truth

Another one of the old poets, whose name has escaped my memory at present, called Truth the daughter of Time.

Aulus Gellius

...For my part, whatever anguish of spirit it might cost, I am willing to know the whole truth; to know the worst, and to provide for it.

Patrick Henry

...the best test of truth is the power of the thought to get itself accepted in the competition of the market, and that truth is the only ground upon which their wishes safely can be carried out.

Oliver Wendell Holmes

We should face reality and our past mistakes in an honest, adult way. Boasting of glory does not make glory, and singing in the dark does not dispel fear.

Hussein, King of Jordan

The most violent revolutions in an individual's beliefs leave most of his old order standing. Time and space, cause and effect, nature and history, and ones own biography remain untouched. New truth is always a go–between, a smoother–over of transitions. It marries old opinion to new fact so as ever to show a minimum of jolt, a maximum of continuity.

William James

The time has come when those sentiments should be uttered and if it is decreed that I should go down because of this speech, then let me go down linked with the truth—let me die in the advocacy of what is just and right.

Abraham Lincoln

You'll never get mixed up if you simply tell the truth.
Then you don't have to remember what you have said,
and you never forget what you have said.

Representative Sam Rayburn

Trying

Ah, but a man's reach should exceed his grasp,
Or what's a heaven for?

Robert Browning

Somebody said that it couldn't be done,
But he with a chuckle replied
That "maybe it couldn't" but he would be one
Who wouldn't say so till he'd tried.
So he buckled right in with the trace of a grin
On his face. If he worried he hid it.
He started to sing as he tackled the thing
That couldn't be done, and he did it.

Edgar A. Guest

The mode in which the inevitable comes to pass is
through effort.

Justice Oliver Wendell Holmes

...It is common sense to take a method and try it; if it
fails, admit it frankly and try another. But above all,
try something. The millions who are in want will not
stand by silently forever while the things to satisfy
their needs are within easy reach.

Franklin D. Roosevelt

Unity

In union there is strength.

Aesop

Unity

Civilisation will not last, freedom will not survive, peace will not be kept, unless a very large majority of mankind unite together to defend them and show themselves possessed of a constabulary power before which barbaric and atavistic forces will stand in awe.

Winston Churchill

All for one, one for all, that is our device, is it not?

Alexandre Dumas

We cannot stand still or slip backwards. We must go forward now together.

Gerald R. Ford

We must all hang together, or most assuredly we shall all *hang separately*.

Attributed to Benjamin Franklin

For the strength of the Pack is the Wolf, and the strength of the Wolf is the Pack.

Rudyard Kipling

Behold, how good and how pleasant it is for brethren to dwell together in unity!

Psalms 133:1–2.

And see the confluence of dreams
That clashed together in our night,
One river born of many streams
Roll in one blaze of blinding light!

George William Russell

Victory

The people who remained victorious were less like conquerors than conquered.

St. Augustine

You ask, what is our aim? I can answer in one word:
It is victory, victory at all costs, victory in spite of all
terror, victory, however long and hard the road may
be; for without victory, there is no survival.

Winston Churchill

No retreat. No retreat. They must conquer or die
who've no retreat.

John Gay

There's an old saying that victory has 100 fathers and
defeat is an orphan.

John F. Kennedy

Beware of rashness, but with energy, and sleepless
vigilance, go forward and give us victories.

Abraham Lincoln

Upon the fields of friendly strife
Are sown the seeds
That, upon other fields, on other days
Will bear the fruits of victory.

General Douglas Macarthur

Be ashamed to die until you have won some victory
for humanity.

Horace Mann

Violence

Violence is as American as cherry pie.

H. Rap Brown

The use of violence as an instrument of persuasion is
therefore inviting and seems to the discontented to be
the only effective protest.

William O. Douglas

Violence

Violence has no constitutional sanction; and every government from the beginning has moved against it. But where grievances pile high and most of the elected spokesmen represent the Establishment, violence may be the only effective response.

William O. Douglas

I'd hate to be in those conditions and I'll tell you if I were in those conditions, you'd have more trouble than you have already because I've got enough spark left in me to lead a mighty good revolt.

Hubert H. Humphrey

The ultimate weakness of violence is that it is a descending spiral, begetting the very thing it seeks to destroy. Instead of diminishing evil, it multiplies it.

Martin Luther King, Jr.

Voting

VOTE. The instrument and symbol of a freeman's power to make a fool of himself and a wreck of his country.

Ambrose Bierce

We'd all like t'vote fer th'best man, but he's never a candidate.

Kin Hubbard

...all who can should vote for the most intelligent, honest, and conscientious men eligible to office, irrespective of former party opinions, who will endeavour to make the new constitutions and the laws passed under them as beneficial as possible to the true interests, prosperity, and liberty of all...

Robert E. Lee

To give the victory to the right, not *bloody bullets*, but *peaceful ballots* only, are necessary,

Abraham Lincoln

I believe that there are societies in which every man may safely be admitted to vote... I say, sir, that there are countries in which the condition of the labouring classes is such that they may safely be intrusted with the right of electing members of the Legislature...

Thomas Babington Macaulay

Bad officials are elected by good citizens who do not vote.

George Jean Nathan

The right of voting for representatives is the primary right by which other rights are protected. To take away this right is to reduce a man to slavery, for slavery consists in being subject to the will of another, and he that has not a vote in the election of representatives is in this case.

Thomas Paine

Perhaps America will one day go fascist democratically, by popular vote.

William L. Shirer

In times of stress and strain, people will vote.

Author Unknown

War

In order for a war to be just, three things are necessary. First, the authority of the sovereign... Secondly, a just cause... Thirdly a rightful intention.

St. Thomas Aquinas

Croesus said to Cambyses; That peace was better than war; because in peace the sons did bury their fathers, but in wars the fathers did bury their sons.

Francis Bacon

I venture to say no war can be long carried on against the will of the people.

Edmund Burke

The eagle has ceased to scream, but the parrots will now begin to chatter. The war of the giants is over and the pigmies will now start to squabble.

Winston Churchill

To jaw–jaw is always better than to war–war.

Winston Churchill

War is not merely a political act but a real political instrument, a continuation of political intercourse, a carrying out of the same by other means.

Karl Von Clausewitz

...war is nothing but a continuation of political intercourse with an admixture of other means.

Karl von Clausewitz

I say when you get into a war, you should win as quick as you can, because your losses become a function of the duration of the war. I believe when you get in a war, get everything you need and win it.

Dwight D. Eisenhower

Nations have recently been led to borrow billions for war; no nation has ever borrowed largely for education. Probably, no nation is rich enough to pay for both war and civilization. We must make our choice; we cannot have both.

Abraham Flexner

All of us who served in one war or another know very well that all wars are the glory and the agony of the young.

Gerald R. Ford

This war, like the next war, is a war to end war.

Attributed to David Lloyd George

Older men declare war. But it is youth that must fight and die. And it is youth who must inherit the tribulation, the sorrow and the triumphs that are the aftermath of war.

Herbert Hoover

Among the calamities of war, may be justly numbered the diminution of the love of truth, by the falsehoods which interest dictates, and credulity encourages.

Samuel Johnson

War is itself a political act with primarily political objects and under the American form of government political officials must necessarily direct its general course.

Captain Dudley W. Knox

Once blood is shed in a national quarrel reason and right are swept aside by the rage of angry men.

David Lloyd George

That's the way it is in war. You win or lose, live or die—and the difference is just an eyelash.

Douglas Macarthur

War contains so much folly, as well as wickedness, that much is to be hoped from the progress of reason; and if any thing is to be hoped, every thing ought to be tried.

James Madison

War

The enemy advances, we retreat; the enemy camps, we harass; the enemy tires, we attack; the enemy retreats, we pursue.

Mao Tse–Tung

War is an ugly thing, but not the ugliest of things: the decayed and degraded state of moral and patriotic feeling which thinks nothing *worth* a war, is worse.

John Stuart Mill

War challenges virtually every other institution of society–the justice and equity of its economy, the adequacy of its political systems, the energy of its productive plant, the bases, wisdom and purposes of its foreign policy.

Walter Millis

A riot is a spontaneous outburst. A war is subject to advance planning.

Richard M. Nixon

Stand your ground. Don't fire unless fired upon, but if they mean to have a war, let it begin here.

John Parker

I have always said that a conference was held for one reason only, to give everybody a chance to get sore at everybody else. Sometimes it takes two or three conferences to scare up a war, but generally one will do it.

Will Rogers

Wars are, of course, as a rule to be avoided; but they are far better than certain kinds of peace.

Theodore Roosevelt

Sometime they'll give a war and nobody will come.

Carl Sandburg

Be convinced that to be happy means to be free and that to be free means to be brave. Therefore do not take lightly the perils of war.

Thucydides

A time will come when a politician who has wilfully made war and promoted international dissension will be as sure of the dock and much surer of the noose than a private homicide. It is not reasonable that those who gamble with men's lives should not stake their own.

H. G. Wells

Since wars begin in the minds of men, it is in the minds of men that the defences of peace must be constructed.

Author unknown.

Weather

For the man sound in body and serene of mind there is no such thing as bad weather! every sky has its beauty, and storms which whip the blood do but make it pulse more vigorously.

George Gissing

We may achieve climate, but weather is thrust upon us.

O. Henry

Climate is theory. Weather is condition.

Oliver Herford

I wonder that any human being should remain in a cold country who could find room in a warm one.

Thomas Jefferson

Weather

When it is evening, ye say, It will be fair weather: for the sky is red. And in the morning, It will be foul weather today: for the sky is red and lowring.

Matthew 16:2-3

The fog comes
  on little cat feet.
It sits looking
  over the harbor and city
    on silent haunches
      and then, moves on.

Carl Sandburg

Winning

If we win, nobody will care. If we lose, there will be nobody to care.

Winston Churchill

I will not only give 'em battle, I will lick 'em!

Richard W. Dowling

You make your own luck, Gig.
You know what makes a good loser? Practice.

Ernest Hemingway

Whoever can surprize well must Conquer.

John Paul Jones

Whether you like it or not, history is on our side. We will bury you.

Nikita S. Khrushchev

For when the One Great Scorer comes
  to mark against your name,
He writes not that you won or lost,
  but how you played the Game.

Grantland Rice

Winning isn't everything, it's the only thing.
Red Sanders

I would rather lose in a cause that will some day win, than win in a cause that will some day lose!
Attributed to Woodrow Wilson

Wisdom

Wise men, though all laws were abolished, would lead the same lives.
Aristophanes

Ask counsel of both times–of the ancient time what is best, and of the latter time what is fittest.
Francis Bacon

Make wisdom your provision for the journey from youth to old age, for it is a more certain support than all other possessions.
Bias

Wisdom don't consist in knowing more that is new, but in knowing less that is false.
Josh Billings

Wisdom too often never comes, and so one ought not to reject it merely because it comes late.
Felix Frankfurter

It is good to meet and drink at the fountains of wisdom inherited from the founding fathers of the Republic.
Warren G. Harding

Whatever the lesson you would convey, be brief, that your hearers may catch quickly what is said and faithfully retain it.
Horace

Wisdom

That which seems the height of absurdity in one generation often becomes the height of wisdom in the next.

Attributed to John Stuart Mill

Pain makes man think. Thought makes man wise. Wisdom makes life endurable.

John Patrick

A man should never be ashamed to own he has been in the wrong, which is but saying, in other words, that he is wiser today than he was yesterday.

Alexander Pope

The fear of the lord is the beginning of wisdom.

Psalms 111:10

When I was a boy of 14, my father was so ignorant I could hardly stand to have the old man around. But when I got to be 21, I was astonished at how much the old man had learned in seven years.

Attributed to Mark Twain

Wisdom is not finally tested in the schools,
Wisdom cannot be passed from one having it
  to another not having it,
Wisdom is of the soul, is not susceptible of proof,
  is its own proof.

Walt Whitman

Wives

Every man who is high up loves to think that he has done it all himself; and the wife smiles, and lets it go at that.

James Matthew Barrie

Rich widows are the only secondhand goods that sell at first–class prices.

Attributed to Benjamin Franklin

An incautious congressman playfully ran his hand over Nick's shiny scalp and commented, "It feels just like my wife's backside." Nick instantly repeated the gesture. "So it does," he replied.

Nicholas Longworth

A man likes his wife to be just clever enough to comprehend his cleverness, and just stupid enough to admire it.

Israel Zangwill

Women

If perticuliar care and attention is not paid to the Laidies we are determined to foment a Rebelion, and will not hold ourselves bound by any Laws in which we have no voice, or Representation.

Abigail Adams

Next to God, we are indebted to women, first for life itself, and then for making it worth having.

C. Nestell Bovee

On one issue, at least, men and women agree: they both distrust women.

H. L. Mencken

Patience makes a woman beautiful in middle age.

Attributed to Ellior Paul

And behind every man who's a *failure* there's a woman, too!

John Ruge

Women

One should never trust a woman who tells one her real age. A woman who would tell one that would tell one anything.

Oscar Wilde

Words

"When *I* use a word," Humpty Dumpty said, in rather a scornful tone, "it means just what I choose it to mean—neither more nor less." "The question is," said Alice, "whether you can make words mean so many different things." "The question is" said Humpty Dumpty, "which is to be master—that's all."

Lewis Carroll

A word is not a crystal, transparent and unchanged, it is the skin of a living thought and may vary greatly in color and content according to the circumstances and the time in which it is used.

Oliver Wendell Holmes

In *Words*, as *Fashions*, the same Rule will hold;
  Alike Fantastick, if *too New, or* Old;
Be not the *first* by whom the *New* are try'd,
  Nor yet the last to lay the Old aside.

Alexander Pope

Work

Nothing is really work unless you would rather be doing something else.

Attributed to James M. Barrie

The most unhappy of all men is the man who cannot tell what he is going to do, who has got no work cut out for him in the world, and does not go into it.

Thomas Carlyle

Our greatest weariness comes from work not done.

Eric Hoffer

I think if I worked for a man I would work for him. I would not work for him a part of the time, and the rest of the time work against him. I would give an undivided service or none. If put to the pinch, an ounce of loyalty is worth a pound of cleverness.

Elbert Hubbard

I long to accomplish a great and noble task, but it is my chief duty to accomplish humble tasks as though they were great and noble. The world is moved along, not only by the mighty shoves of its heroes, but also by the aggregate of the tiny pushes of each honest worker.

Attributed to Helen Keller

As good play for nothing, you know, as work for nothing.

Walter Scott

You must obey this now for a Law, that he that will not worke shall not eate (except by sicknesse he be disabled:) for the labours, of thirtie or fortie honest and industrious men shall not be consumed to maintaine an hundred and fiftie idle loyterers.

John Smith

Drive a nail home and clinch it so faithfully that you can wake up in the night and think of your work with satisfaction a work at which you would not be ashamed to invoke the Muse.

Henry David Thoreau

World

Give me matter, and I will construct a world out of it!
Immanuel Kant

The world is large,
  when its weary leagues two loving hearts divide;
But the world is small,
  when your enemy is loose on the other side.
John Boyle O'reilly

We have it in our power to begin the world over again.
Thomas Paine

The world of the future will not flourish behind walls—no matter who builds them and no matter what their purpose. A world divided economically must inevitably be a world divided politically. As Secretary of State, I cannot contemplate that prospect with anything but deep disquiet.
William P. Rogers

Physicists and astronomers see their own implications in the world being round, but to me it means that only one-third of the world is asleep at any given time and the other two-thirds is up to something.
Dean Rusk

Writing

When that passage was written only God and Robert Browning understood it. Now only God understands it.

Rudolf Besier

I don't wait for moods. You accomplish nothing if you do that. Your mind must know it has got to get down to work.

Pearl Buck

The original style is not the style which never borrows of any one, but that which no other person is capable of reproducing.

François René de Chateaubriand

Writing a long and substantial book is like having a friend and companion at your side, to whom you can always turn for comfort and amusement, and whose society becomes more attractive as a new and widening field of interest is lighted in the mind.

Winston Churchill

If I let my fingers wander idly over the keys of a type-writer it might happen that my screed made an intelligible sentence. If an army of monkeys were strumming on typewriters they might write all the books in the British Museum.

Arthur S. Eddington

Composition is for the most part, an effort of slow diligence and steady perseverence, to which the mind is dragged by necessity or resolution.

Samuel Johnson

The impulse to create beauty is rather rare in literary men... Far ahead of it comes the yearning to make money. And after the yearning to make money comes the yearning to make a noise.

H. L. Mencken

Writing

If you steal from one author, it's plagiarism. If you steal from two, it's research.

Wilson Mizner

The present letter is a very long one, simply because I had no leisure to make it shorter.

Blaise Pascal

Fine writers should split hairs together, and sit side by side, like friendly apes, to pick the fleas from each other's fur.

Logan Pearsall Smith

Originality is nothing but judicious imitation. The most original writers borrowed one from another. The instruction we find in books is like fire. We fetch it from our neighbor's, kindle it at home, communicate it to others, and it becomes the property of all.

Attributed to Voltaire

Youth

I pray for no more youth
To perish before its prime;
That Revenge and iron–heated War
May fade with all that has gone before
Into the night of time.

Aeschylus

I'm youth, I'm joy, I'm a little bird that has broken out of the egg.

James M. Barrie

Tell me what are the prevailing sentiments that occupy the minds of your young men, and I will tell you what is to be the character of the next generation.

Attributed to Edmund Burke

The young leading the young, is like the blind leading the blind; "they will both fall into the ditch."

Lord Chesterfield

Young men are as apt to think themselves wise enough, as drunken men are to think themselves sober enough.

Lord Chesterfield

Twenty to twenty–five! These are the years! Don't be content with things as they are. . . . Don't take No for an answer. Never submit to failure. Do not be fobbed off with mere personal success or acceptance. You will make all kinds of mistakes; but as long as you are generous and true, and also fierce, you cannot hurt the world or even seriously distress her. She was made to be wooed and won by youth. She has lived and thrived only by repeated subjugations.

Winston Churchill

Let them be assured that it is not the last word. But before they blame, as blame they should, these callow ill–tutored youths, they must be sure that they have not been set a bad example by people much older and much higher up.

Winston Churchill

Truthfulness is a cornerstone in character, and if it be not firmly laid in youth, there will ever after be a weak spot in the foundation.

jefferson davis

It is easy for a youngster to go wrong from hastiness and lack of thought.

Robert Fitzgerald

Youth

Thou dost know
The faults to which the young are ever prone;
The will is quick to act, the judgment weak

Robert Graves

Through our great good fortune, in our youth our hearts were touched with fire. It was given to us to learn at the outset that life is a profound and passionate thing.

Oliver Wendell Holmes

Thou know'st the o'er–eager vehemence of youth,
How quick in temper, and in judgement weak.

Homer

It is very natural for young men to be vehement, acrimonious and severe. For as they seldom comprehend at once all the consequences of a position, or perceive the difficulties by which cooler and more experienced reasoners are restrained from confidence, they form their conclusions with great precipitance. Seeing nothing that can darken or embarrass the question, they expect to find their own opinion universally prevalent, and are inclined to impute uncertainty and hesitation to want of honesty, rather than of knowledge.

Samuel Johnson

Nothing matters more to the future of this Nation than insuring that our young men and women learn to believe in themselves and believe in their dreams, and that they develop this capacity—that you develop this capacity, so that you keep it all of your lives.

Richard M. Nixon

Youth is a wonderful thing. What a crime to waste it on children.

Attributed to George Bernard Shaw

Youth, which is forgiven everything, forgives itself nothing: age, which forgives itself everything, is forgiven nothing.

George Bernard Shaw

Youth is not a time of life–it is a state of mind. It is not a matter of red cheeks, red lips and supple knees. It is a temper of the will; a quality of the imagination; a vigor of the emotions; it is a freshness of the deep springs of life.

Samuel Ullman

The most conservative persons I ever met are college undergraduates. The radicals are the men past middle life.

Woodrow Wilson

Index of Topics

317

Get 2 Free Books,
Plus 2 Free Gifts -
just for trying the Reader Service!

STRS17R